Teacher's Resource Masters

VOLUME 2

Topics 9–14

Interactive Math Stories
Home-School Connection Letters
Math and Science Activities
Daily Common Core Review
Reteach to Build Understanding
Center Games
Teaching Tools

enVisionmath® 2.0
SCOTT FORESMAN · ADDISON WESLEY

PEARSON

Glenview, Illinois • Boston, Massachusetts • Chandler, Arizona • Hoboken, New Jersey

ISBN-13:   978-0-328-82756-5
ISBN-10:   0-328-82756-8

7   17

Grade K
Volume 2: Topics 9–14

Topic 13 **Analyze, Compare, and Create Shapes**

Topic 14 **Describe and Compare Measurable Attributes**

This book belongs to:

_____

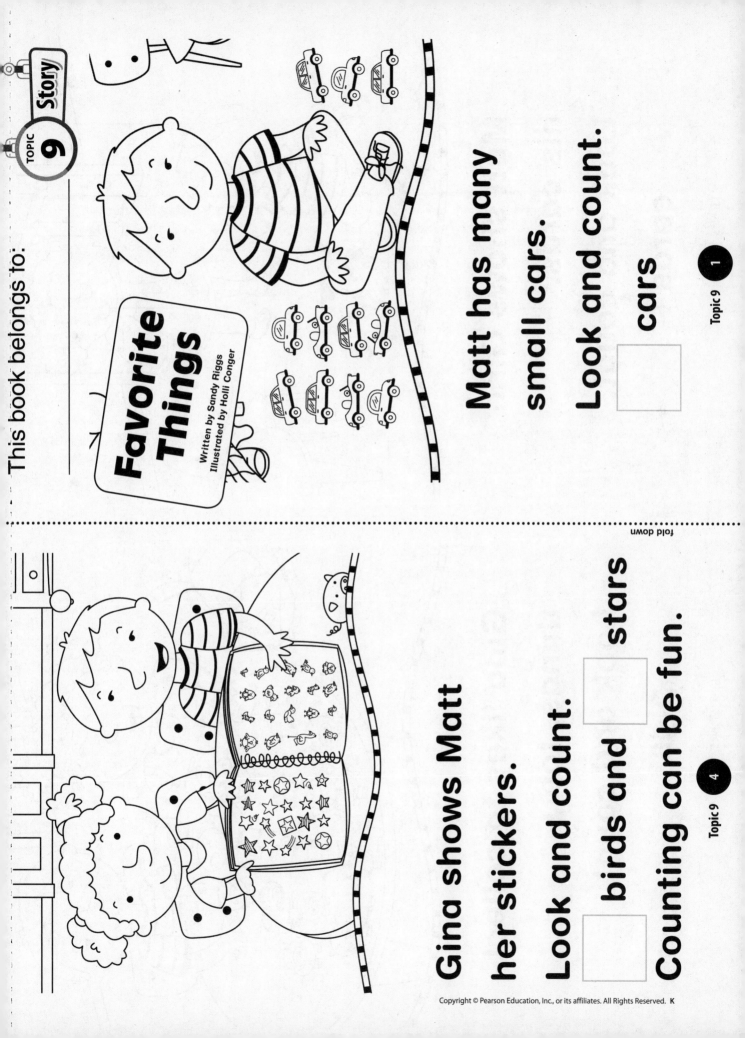

Favorite Things

Written by Sandy Riggs
Illustrated by Holli Conger

Matt has many
small cars.
Look and count.

cars

Topic 9 **1**

Gina shows Matt
her stickers.
Look and count.

birds and stars

Counting can be fun.

Topic 9 **4**

fold down

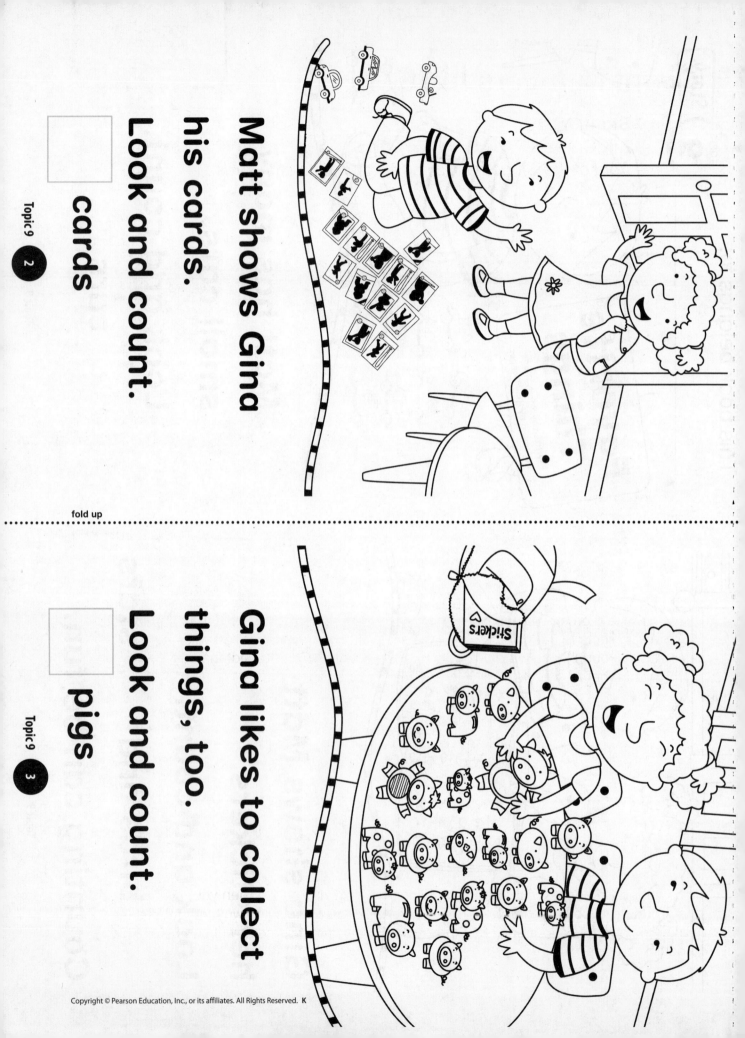

Look and count.

Matt shows Gina

his cards.

cards

fold up

Look and count.

Gina likes to collect

things, too.

Stickers

pigs

Name _____

Count Numbers to 20

Topic 9 Standards
K.CC.A.2, K.CC.A.3, K.CC.B.4c, K.CC.B.5
See the front of the Student's Edition for complete standards.

Dear Family,

Your child is learning to count, read, and write numbers from 11 through 20. He or she will learn to count forward from any number to 20. Your child will also learn to use logical reasoning to solve problems when there is more than one possible solution.

Count and Write
Each number word has its own unique symbol.

16 ⬤⬤⬤⬤⬤⬤⬤⬤⬤⬤ ⬤⬤⬤⬤⬤⬤
17 ⬤⬤⬤⬤⬤⬤⬤⬤⬤⬤ ⬤⬤⬤⬤⬤⬤⬤
18 ⬤⬤⬤⬤⬤⬤⬤⬤⬤⬤ ⬤⬤⬤⬤⬤⬤⬤⬤
19 ⬤⬤⬤⬤⬤⬤⬤⬤⬤⬤ ⬤⬤⬤⬤⬤⬤⬤⬤⬤
20 ⬤⬤⬤⬤⬤⬤⬤⬤⬤⬤ ⬤⬤⬤⬤⬤⬤⬤⬤⬤⬤

Try this activity with your child to practice counting objects and counting forward from any number to 20.

Make a Group of Objects

Use 20 small objects such as pennies, buttons, paper clips, or paper squares. Ask your child to make a group with 15 objects and write the number 15 on a piece of paper. Then add objects to the group one at a time as you count forward to 20 with your child. Finally, ask your child to write the numbers you counted. Then repeat the activity with a different number of objects.

Observe Your Child

Focus on Mathematical Practice 7
Look for and make use of structure.

Help your child become proficient with Mathematical Practice 7. When your child makes the group of 15 objects, ask him or her to organize the objects in a way that makes them easier to count. Ask your child to explain what a ten-frame is and how it can help to organize objects.

Contar números hasta 20

Estándares del Tema 9
K.CNC.A.2, K.CNC.A.3, K.CNC.B.4c, K.CNC.B.5
Los estándares completos se encuentran en las páginas preliminares del
Libro del estudiante.

Estimada familia:

Su niño(a) está aprendiendo a contar, leer y escribir números del 11 al 20. Él o ella
aprenderá a contar hacia adelante desde cualquier número hasta el 20. Su niño(a)
también aprenderá a usar el razonamiento lógico para resolver problemas cuando hay
más de una solución posible.

Contar y escribir
Cada número en palabras tiene su propio símbolo.

16 ⃝⃝⃝⃝⃝⃝⃝⃝⃝⃝ ⃝⃝⃝⃝⃝⃝
17 ⃝⃝⃝⃝⃝⃝⃝⃝⃝⃝ ⃝⃝⃝⃝⃝⃝⃝
18 ⃝⃝⃝⃝⃝⃝⃝⃝⃝⃝ ⃝⃝⃝⃝⃝⃝⃝⃝
19 ⃝⃝⃝⃝⃝⃝⃝⃝⃝⃝ ⃝⃝⃝⃝⃝⃝⃝⃝⃝
20 ⃝⃝⃝⃝⃝⃝⃝⃝⃝⃝ ⃝⃝⃝⃝⃝⃝⃝⃝⃝⃝

Intente esta actividad con su niño(a) para practicar el conteo de objetos y el conteo hacia
adelante desde cualquier número hasta el 20.

Formar un grupo de objetos

Use 20 objetos pequeños como monedas de 1¢, botones, clips o cuadrados de papel.
Pídale a su niño(a) que forme un grupo con 15 objetos y escriba el número 15 en una
hoja de papel. Luego, añada objetos al grupo, uno a la vez, mientras cuenta hacia
adelante hasta el 20 con su niño. Por último, pídale a su niño(a) que escriba los números
que contaron. Luego, repita la actividad con un número diferente de objetos.

Observe a su niño(a)

Enfoque en la Práctica matemática 7:
Buscar y utilizar la estructura.

Ayude a su niño(a) a adquirir competencia en la Práctica matemática 7. Cuando su niño(a)
forme el grupo de 15 objetos, pídale que organice los objetos de manera que sean más
fáciles de contar. Pídale a su niño(a) que explique qué es un marco de 10 y cómo le puede
servir de ayuda para organizar los objetos.

Shelters

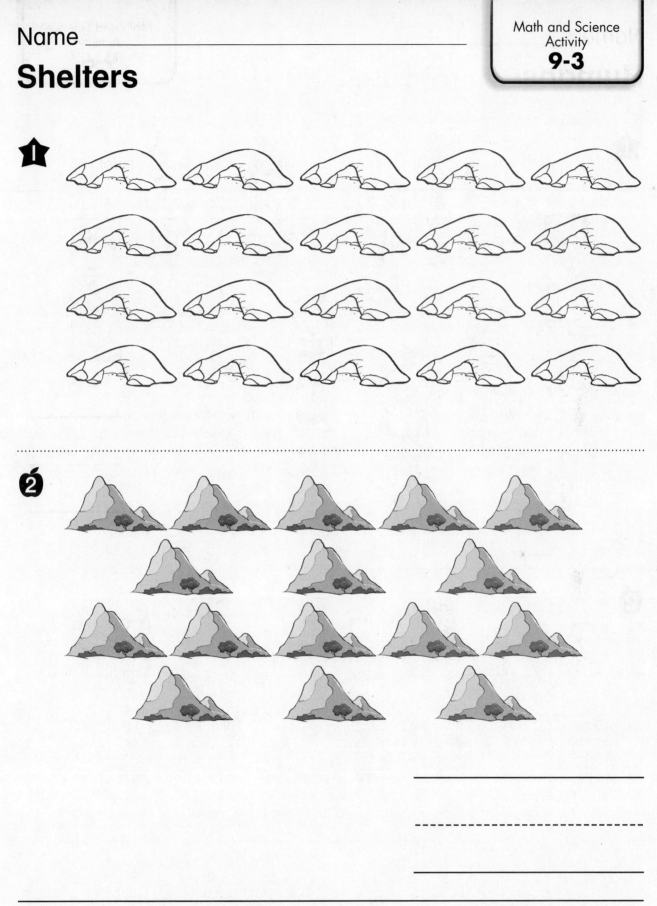

Directions Say: *Did you know that all living things need shelter in order to survive, no matter how big or small they are?*
Have students: count and color 17 caves; ❷ count the ant hills, draw a group of counters with the same number, and
then practice writing the number that tells how many counters. **Extension** Draw a group of 16 animal homes and another
group of 17 animal homes, and then practice writing the numbers that tell how many.

Math and Science Activity 9·3

Humans

Directions Say: *People, like all living things, are organisms. An organism is any living thing that can function on its own. This includes your pet, the tree in your backyard, and you!* Have students: ❶ count the children, and then write the number that tells how many; ❷ draw a circle around the group that has 10 children. **Extension** Have students draw a group of 10 organisms, and a group of 5 organisms. Then have them draw a circle around the group that has ten.

1

A 10

B 9

C 8

D 7

2

0   1   5   10

A   B   C   D

3

_____   _____

- - - - - - - - - -   - - - - - - - - - -

_____   _____

Directions Have students: **1** mark the number that tells how many spoons; **2** mark the number that tells how many muffins; **3** count the toys in each group, and then write the numbers that tell how many of each kind of toy.

 D 9·1

Name _____

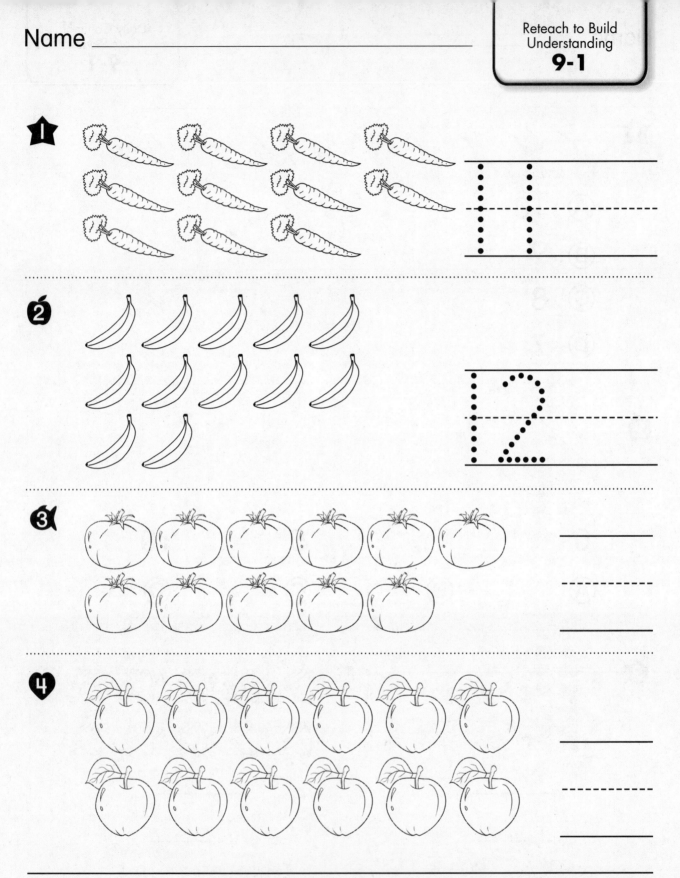

Directions Say: ⭐ *Look at the group of carrots. Let's count them together. There are **eleven** carrots. Eleven is a group of ten and one more. Practice writing the number that tells how many;* ❷ *Let's count the group of bananas. There are 12 bananas. Twelve is a group of ten and two more. Practice writing the number that tells how many;* ❸ *How many tomatoes are there? Write the number that tells how many;* ❹ *How many apples are there? Write the number that tells how many.* **On the Back!** *Have students draw groups of 11 or 12 objects, and then practice writing the number that tells how many.*

Play a Game

Start 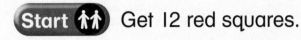 Get 12 red squares.

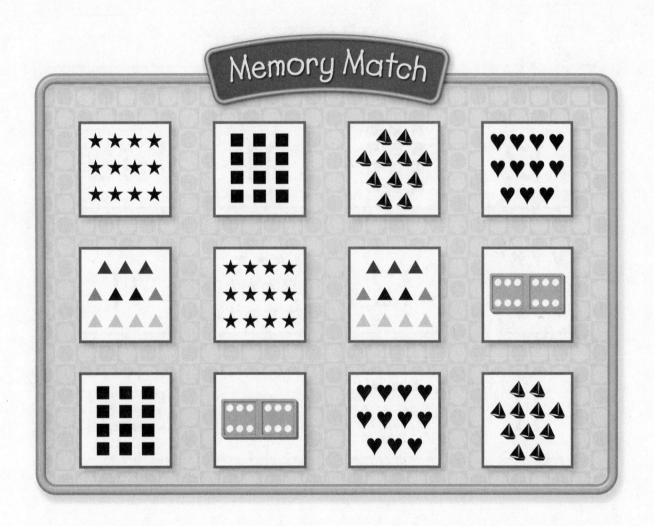

Memory Match

Materials	12 red squares
Oral Directions	**TRY** Before the game begins, cover each picture with a red square. Take turns. On your turn, uncover two game spaces. If the pictures are the same, count the number of objects in one picture. Trace that number in the air. Say it out loud. Keep the 2 red squares. If the pictures are different, put the squares back where they were. Play until all the pictures are uncovered. At the end of the game, count your squares. If you have more squares, you win.

TRY AGAIN If you have time, play again! |

Center Game ★ 9·1

Play a Game

Start  Get 12 red squares.

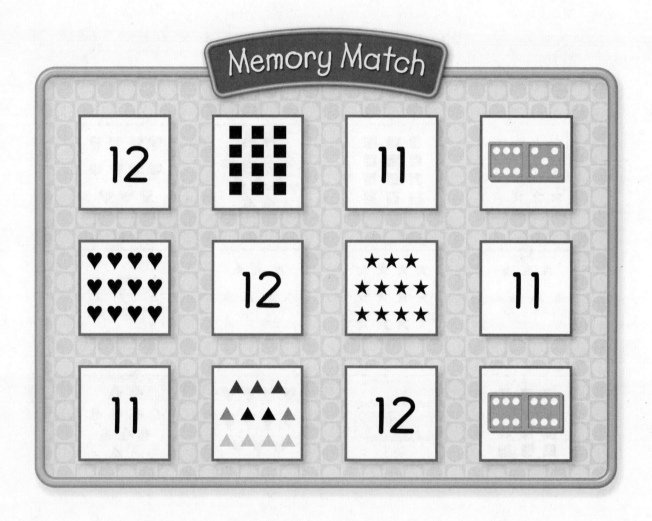

Memory Match

Materials   12 red squares

Oral Directions   **TRY** Before the game begins, cover each game space with a red square. Take turns. On your turn, uncover two game spaces. If you see one picture and a number that shows how many are in that picture, explain why. Trace the number in the air. Say it out loud. Keep the 2 red squares. If you do NOT see a picture and a number that shows how many are in that picture, put the squares back where they were. Play until all the pictures are uncovered. At the end of the game, count your squares. If you have more squares, you win.

TRY AGAIN If you have time, play again!

Name _____

1

9   10   11   12

Ⓐ   Ⓑ   Ⓒ   Ⓓ

2

Ⓐ 9

Ⓑ 10

Ⓒ 11

Ⓓ 12

3

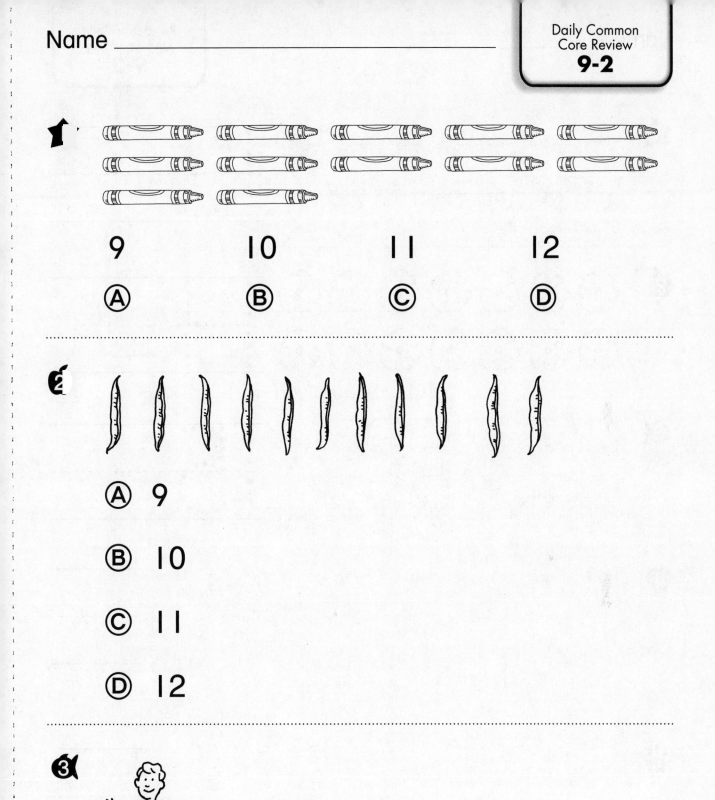

Directions Have students: **1** mark the number that tells how many crayons; **2** mark the number that tells how many string beans; **3** draw Jerry's 11 bouncy balls.

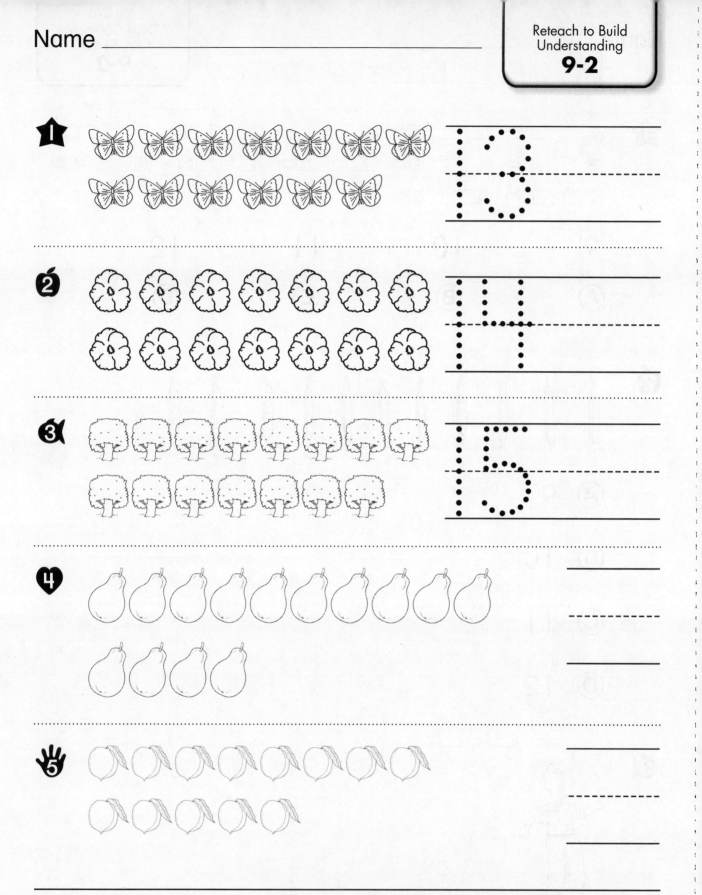

Directions Say: ⭐ *Look at the butterflies. Let's count them. There are* **thirteen** *butterflies. Practice writing the number 13;* ② *Let's count the flowers. There are 14 flowers. Practice writing the number 14;* ③ *Let's count the trees. There are 15 trees. Practice writing the number 15;* ④ *How many pears are there? Write the number that tells how many;* ✋ *How many peaches are there? Write the number that tells how many.* **On the Back!** Have students draw a picture to show a group of 15 objects, and then practice writing the number that tells how many.

Helping Hands

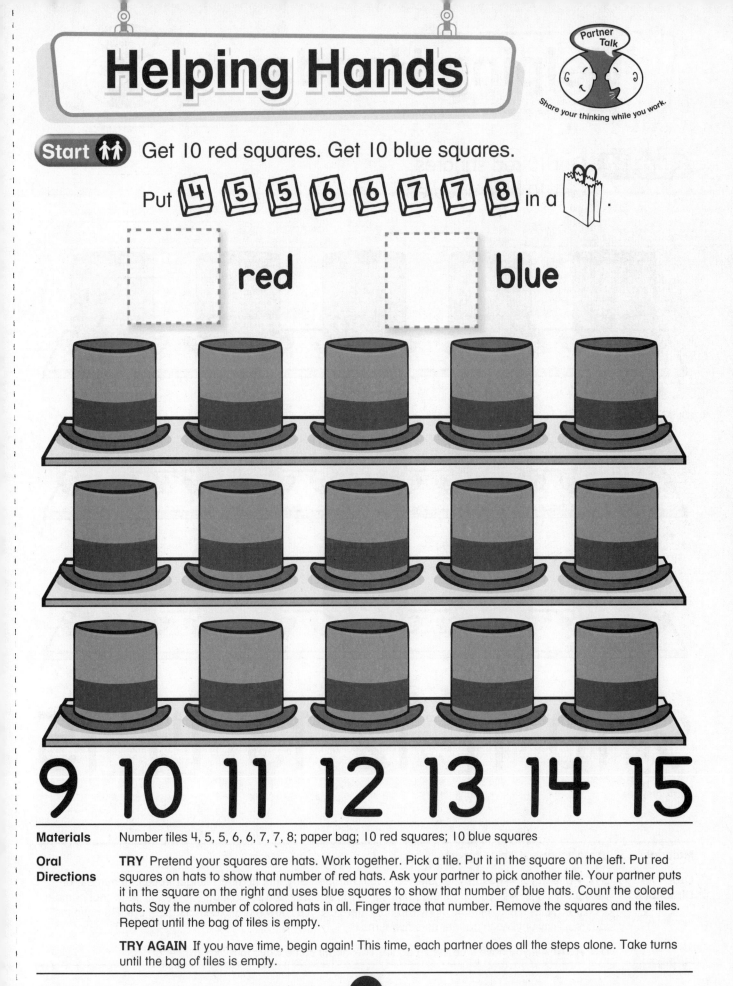

Partner Talk — Share your thinking while you work.

Start 👥 Get 10 red squares. Get 10 blue squares.

Put 4 5 5 6 6 7 7 8 in a 🛍.

⬜ **red**   ⬜ **blue**

9 10 11 12 13 14 15

Materials Number tiles 4, 5, 5, 6, 6, 7, 7, 8; paper bag; 10 red squares; 10 blue squares

Oral Directions **TRY** Pretend your squares are hats. Work together. Pick a tile. Put it in the square on the left. Put red squares on hats to show that number of red hats. Ask your partner to pick another tile. Your partner puts it in the square on the right and uses blue squares to show that number of blue hats. Count the colored hats. Say the number of colored hats in all. Finger trace that number. Remove the squares and the tiles. Repeat until the bag of tiles is empty.

TRY AGAIN If you have time, begin again! This time, each partner does all the steps alone. Take turns until the bag of tiles is empty.

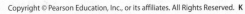

Center Game ★ 9·2

Helping Hands

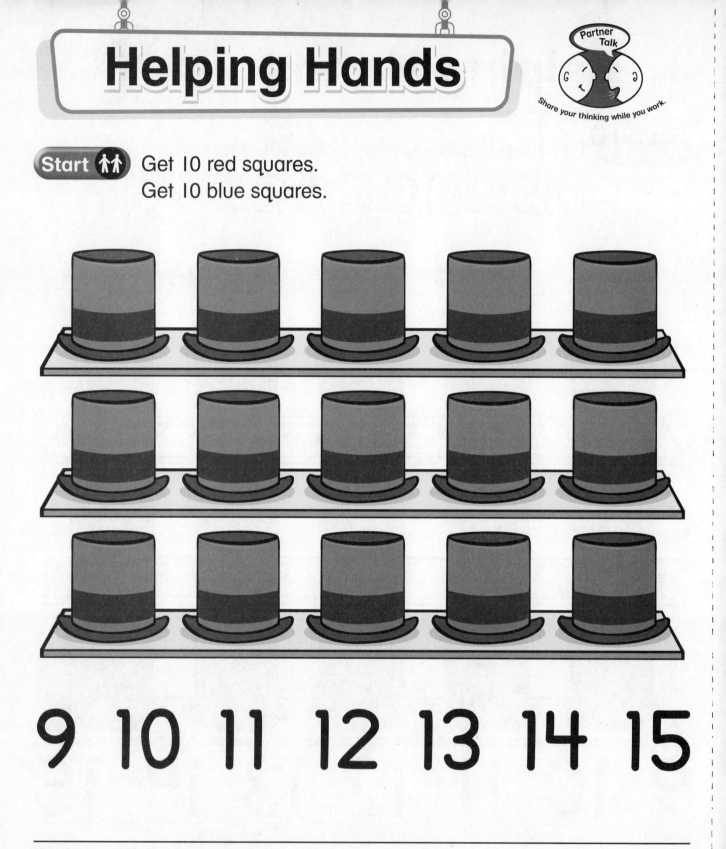

Start 👥 Get 10 red squares.
Get 10 blue squares.

9 10 11 12 13 14 15

Materials   10 red squares, 10 blue squares

Oral Directions   **TRY** Pretend your squares are hats. Point to a number. Say that number. Finger trace that number on the activity page. Ask your partner to use some red squares and some blue squares to show that number of colored hats in all. Tell how many red hats there are. Tell how many blue hats there are. Remove the squares. Play until each partner gets five turns.

TRY AGAIN If you have time, begin again! Talk about some ways to make 13, 14, or 15.

Name _____

⭐ $10 = 7 + $ ----------

       2   3   4   5

   Ⓐ   Ⓑ   Ⓒ   Ⓓ

❷

Ⓐ 11

Ⓑ 12

Ⓒ 13

Ⓓ 14

❸

_____

_____

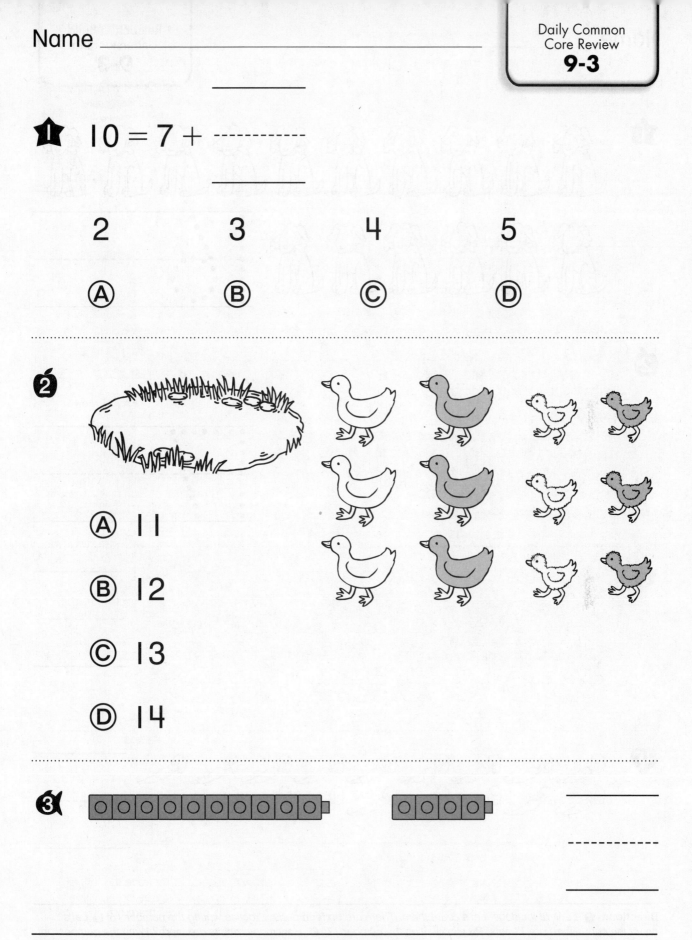

Directions Have students: ⭐ find the missing part of 10, and then mark the number that completes the equation;
❷ mark the number that tells how many ducks; ❸ count the cubes, and then write the number that tells how many in all.

D 9·3

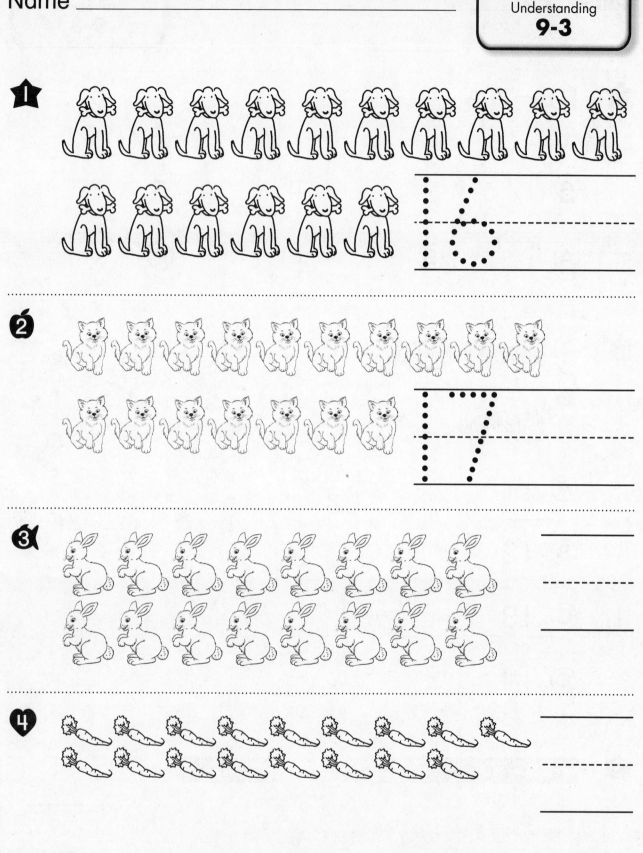

1

2

3

4

Directions ⭐ *Look at the dogs. Let's count them. There are* **sixteen** *dogs. Practice writing the number 16;* 🍎 *Let's count the cats. There are 17 cats. Practice writing the number 17;* ❸ *How many rabbits are there? Write the number that tells how many;* ❤ *How many carrots are there? Write the number that tells how many.* **On the Back!** *Have students draw a picture to show a group of 16 or 17 objects, and then practice writing the number that tells how many.*

Name _____

1 ⭐

(A) 17

(B) 16

(C) 15

(D) 14

2

_____

- - - - - - - -

_____

Directions Have students: ⭐ mark the number that tells how many trees; count the hats, and then write the number that tells how many.

1 ☆

18

2 🍎

19

3 🐋

20

4 ♥

5 ✋

Directions Say: ☆ *Look at the sea horses. Let's count them. There are* **eighteen** *sea horses. Practice writing the number 18;* 🍎 *Let's count the fish. There are 19 fish. Practice writing the number 19;* 🐋 *Let's count the eels. There are 20 eels. Practice writing the number 20;* ♥ *How many fish hooks are there? Write the number that tells how many;* ✋ *How many alligators are there? Write the number that tells how many.* **On the Back!** *Have students draw a picture to show a group of 20 counters, and then practice writing the number that tells how many.*

R 9·4

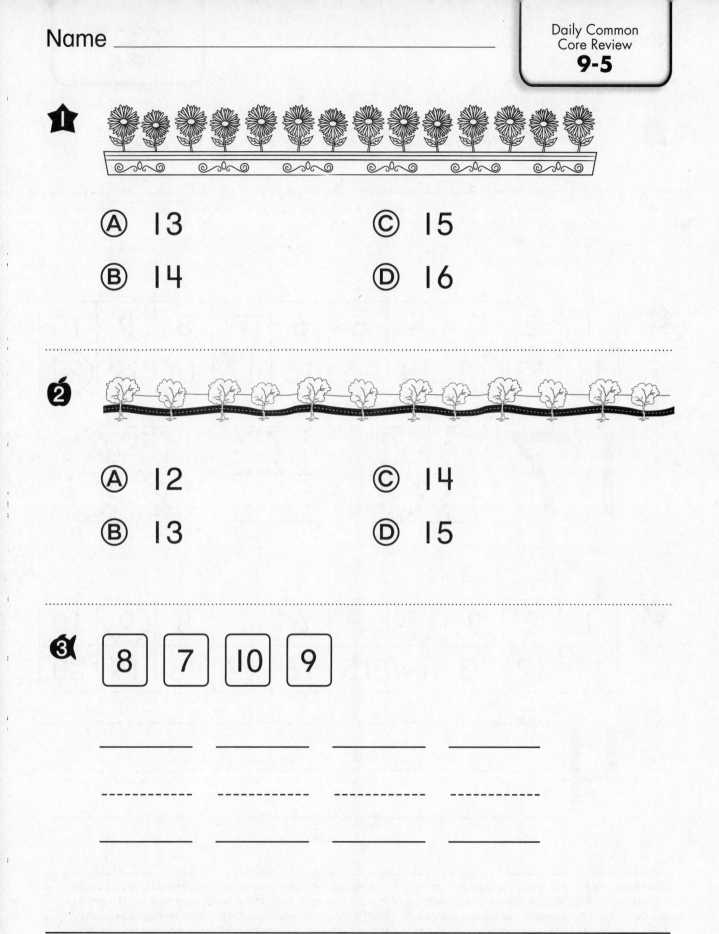

⭐ 1

Ⓐ 13   Ⓒ 15

Ⓑ 14   Ⓓ 16

⭐ 2

Ⓐ 12   Ⓒ 14

Ⓑ 13   Ⓓ 15

⭐ 3

| 8 | 7 | 10 | 9 |

_____   _____   _____   _____

- - - - - - -   - - - - - - -   - - - - - - -   - - - - - - -

_____   _____   _____   _____

Directions Have students: ⭐1 mark the number that tells how many daisies; ⭐2 mark the number that tells how many trees; ⭐3 write the smallest number, and then count forward and write the number that is 1 greater than the number before.

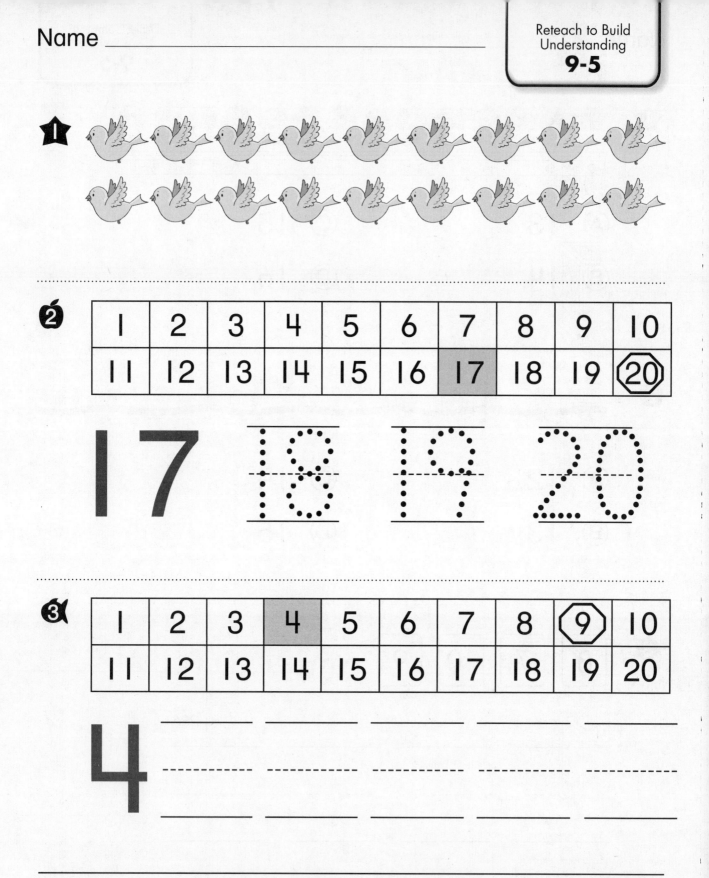

⭐ 🐦 🐦 🐦 🐦 🐦 🐦 🐦 🐦 🐦
🐦 🐦 🐦 🐦 🐦 🐦 🐦 🐦 🐦

❷

1	2	3	4	5	6	7	8	9	10
11	12	13	14	15	16	17	18	19	20

17   18   19   20

❸

1	2	3	4	5	6	7	8	9	10
11	12	13	14	15	16	17	18	19	20

4 ___ ___ ___ ___ ___

Directions ⭐ Point to each **row** of birds. Say: *How many rows of birds are there?* Have students draw a circle around the top row of birds. ❷ Say: *Point to the bottom row of the number chart. Point to the highlighted number. What is that number? Count forward until you reach the stop sign. What numbers did you count? Write each number you counted.* ❸ Have students find the highlighted number on the number chart, count forward until they reach the stop sign, and then write each number they counted. **On the Back!** Have students write the number 12, count forward until they reach 16, and then write the numbers they counted.

Listen and Learn

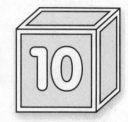

Partner Talk

Share your thinking while you work.

Start 🧍🧍 Get 1 blue square.

1   2   3   4   5

6   7   8   9   10

    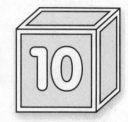
11   12   13   14   15

16   17   18   19   20

Materials	1 blue square
Oral Directions	**TRY** Count the blocks. Ask your partner to finger trace each number in order as you count aloud. Then let your partner count aloud as you finger trace the numbers in order.
	TRY AGAIN If you have time, take turns. Place the blue square on any number. Ask your partner to count forward to 20 from the blue square. Take turns until each partner gets five turns.

Center Game ★ 9·5

Listen and Learn

Start 👥 Get 1 blue square.
Get 20 red squares.

Materials   1 blue square, 20 red squares

Oral Directions

TRY Take turns. Place a blue square on a number. Place a red square on another number that follows it. Ask your partner to count forward from the blue square and stop at the red square. Take turns until each of you gets five turns.

TRY AGAIN If you have time, take turns and play again. Show some red squares. Count the squares. Count aloud. Ask your partner to count the same number of bears in order beginning with 1.

Name _____

1

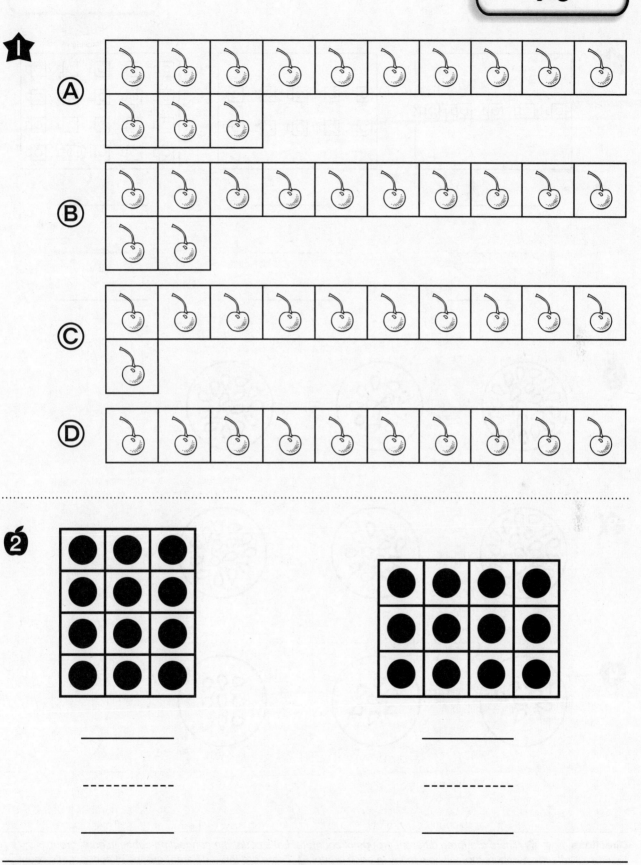

2

_____   _____

- - - - - - - - -   - - - - - - - -

_____   _____

Directions Have students: **1** mark the picture that shows 11 cherries; **2** count the counters in each group, and then write the numbers that tell how many.

Name _____

1

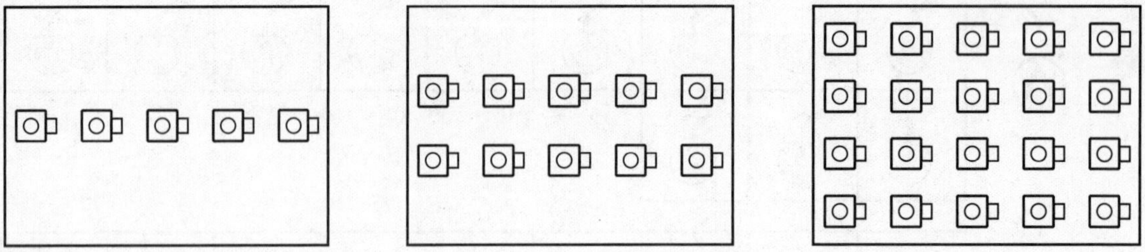

_____   _____   _____

- - - - - - - -   - - - - - - - - - -   - - - - - - - - - -

_____   _____   _____

2

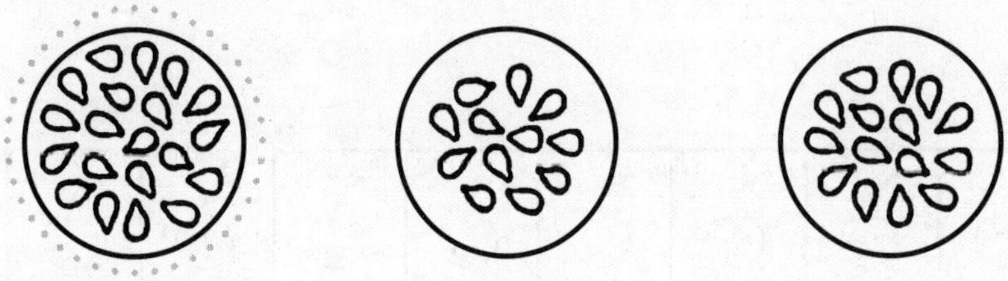

3

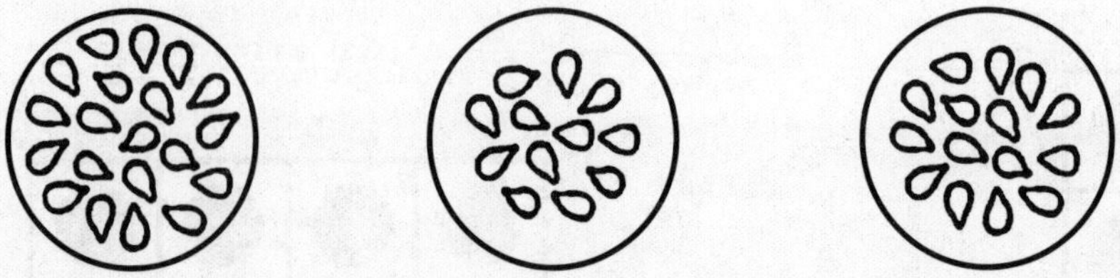

4

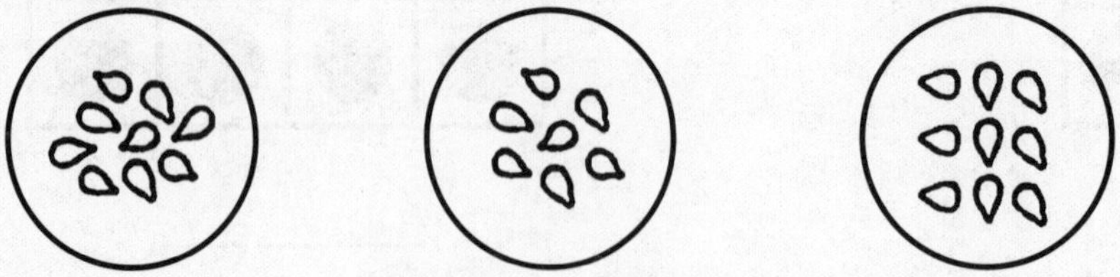

Directions Say: 1 *There are three different groups of counters. Let's count the connecting cubes in each group together. Write the numbers that tell how many in each group;* 2 *There are three different groups of seeds. Let's count the seeds on each plate. Which plate has 20 seeds? Draw a circle around that plate.* Have students: 3 *draw a circle around the plate that has 12 seeds;* 4 *draw a circle around the 2 plates that have 9 seeds.*

⭐ 7 + 2 = ---------- _____

| 5 | 6 | 8 | 9 |
| Ⓐ | Ⓑ | Ⓒ | Ⓓ |

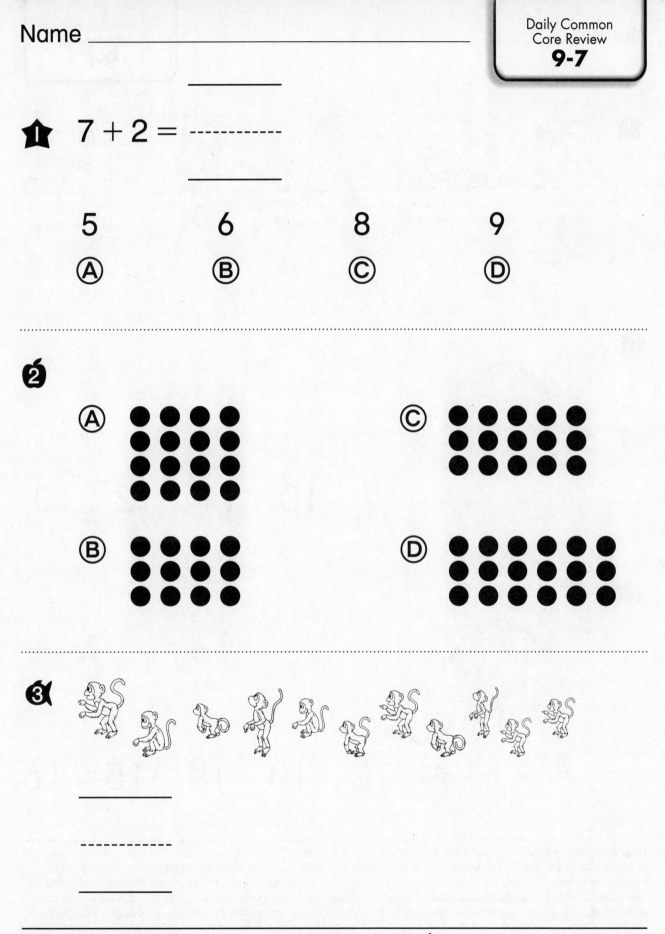

🍎**2**

Ⓐ   Ⓒ

Ⓑ   Ⓓ

⭐**3**

_____

_____

Directions Have students: ⭐ mark the number that completes the equation; 🍎 mark the picture that shows 18 counters; ⭐ count the monkeys, and then write the number that tells how many.

D 9·7

Name _____

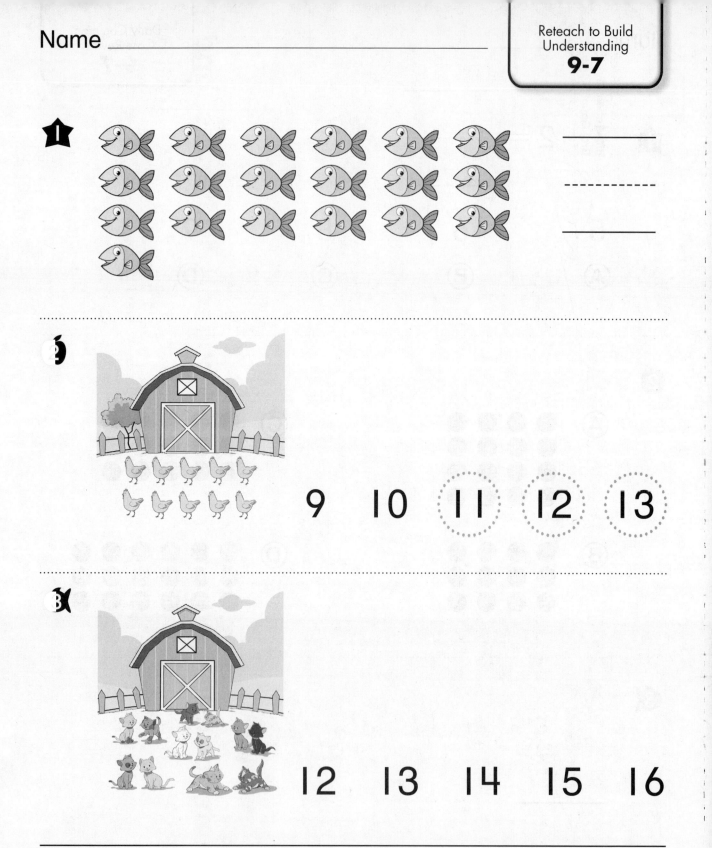

1

2   9   10   (11)   (12)   (13)

3   12   13   14   15   16

Directions Say: **1** *Let's count the fish together. There are **nineteen** fish. Write the number that tells how many;* **2** *Look at the picture of the farm. There are more than 9 chickens on a farm. Some chickens are outside the barn. 1 or more chickens are inside the barn. How many chickens are outside of the barn? If there are 1 or more chickens inside the barn, how many chickens could be inside the barn? Draw a circle around the numbers that tell how many chickens there could be in all;* **3** *There are more than 10 kittens on the farm. Some kittens are outside the barn. 0, 1, or 2 kittens are inside the barn. Count the kittens outside the barn, and then draw a circle around the numbers that tell how many kittens there could be in all.* **On the Back!** *Have students draw from 9 to 12 objects. Have them write the number to tell how many, and then write the next three numbers.*

R 9·7

This book belongs to:

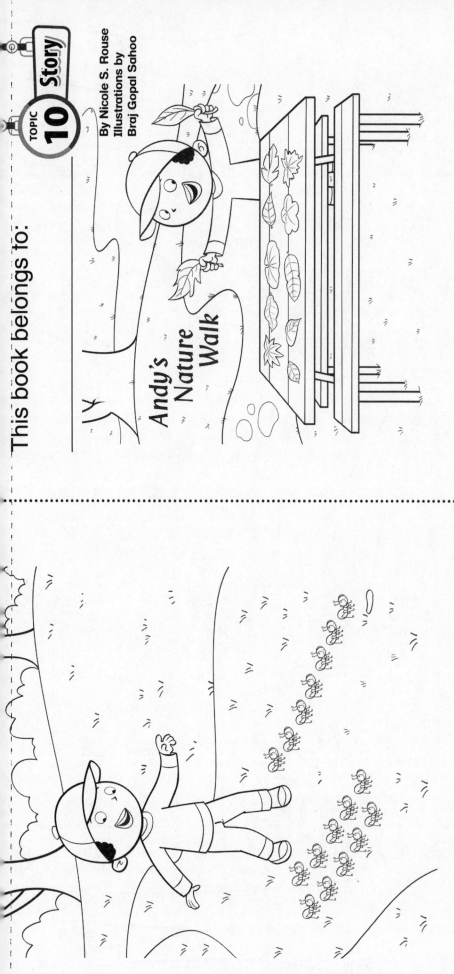

Andy's Nature Walk

By Nicole S. Rouse
Illustrations by Braj Gopal Sahoo

Andy collects 10 leaves, and then he collects some more. How many leaves does he collect in all?

10 + ___ = ___

Topic 10 · 1

fold down

Andy counts 10 ants, and then he counts some more. How many ants does he count in all?

10 + ___ = ___

Topic 10 · 4

Andy finds 10 rocks, and
then he finds some more.
How many rocks does he
find in all?

10 + ___ = ___

fold up

Andy chases 10 butterflies,
and then he chases
some more.
How many butterflies
does he chase in all?

10 + ___ = ___

Name _____

Compose and Decompose Numbers 11 to 19

Topic 10 Standard
K.NBT.A.1
See the front of the Student's Edition for complete standards.

Dear Family,

Your child is learning about composing and decomposing numbers. In this topic, he or she will learn to compose and decompose numbers 11 to 19. Your child will learn ways to show these numbers as the sum of 10 ones and some more ones. He or she will also learn to write equations to show these numbers in different ways.

Compose and Decompose Numbers
You can show numbers in different ways. The ten-frame and equations show 12 as 10 and 2 more.

$10 + 2 = 12$

$12 = 10 + 2$

Here is an activity to do with your child to practice composing and decomposing numbers 11 to 19.

10 and More Ones

Give your child 19 pennies and a sheet of paper with a ten-frame drawn on it. Say a number from 11 to 19. Have your child fill the ten-frame first with pennies, and then count on from 10 to the number you said. Then have him or her say the number both as 10 and ____ ones and as an equation. Repeat with other numbers.

Observe Your Child

Focus on Mathematical Practice 3:
Construct viable arguments and critique the reasoning of others.

Help your child become proficient with Mathematical Practice 3. After your child says the equation, ask him or her to explain how he or she knows the equation is correct.

Componer y descomponer números del 11 al 19

Estándar del Tema 10

K.NBD.A.1

Los estándares completos se encuentran en las páginas preliminares del
Libro del estudiante.

Estimada familia:

Su niño(a) está aprendiendo a componer y descomponer números. En este tema, aprenderá a componer y descomponer números del 11 al 19. Su niño(a) aprenderá maneras de mostrar estos números como la suma de 10 unidades y algunas unidades más. También aprenderá a escribir ecuaciones para mostrar esos números de diferentes maneras.

Componer y descomponer números
Los números se pueden mostrar de diferentes maneras. El marco de 10 y las ecuaciones muestran 12 como 10 y 2 más.

$10 + 2 = 12$

$12 = 10 + 2$

Esta es una actividad que puede hacer con su niño(a) para practicar la composición y descomposición de números del 11 al 19.

---

10 y más unidades

Dé a su niño(a) 19 monedas de 1¢ y una hoja de papel con un marco de 10 dibujado. Diga un número del 11 al 19. Pídale a su niño(a) que primero rellene el marco de 10 con las monedas de 1¢ y que luego cuente hacia adelante desde el 10 hasta el número que usted le dijo. Luego, pídale que diga el número como 10 y ____ unidades y como una ecuación. Repita con otros números.

Observe a su niño(a)

Enfoque en la Práctica matemática 3:
Construir argumentos viables y evaluar el razonamiento de otros.

Ayude a su niño(a) a adquirir competencia en la Práctica matemática 3. Luego de que su niño(a) diga la ecuación, pídale que explique cómo sabe que la ecuación es correcta.

Name _____

Shelter from Sunlight

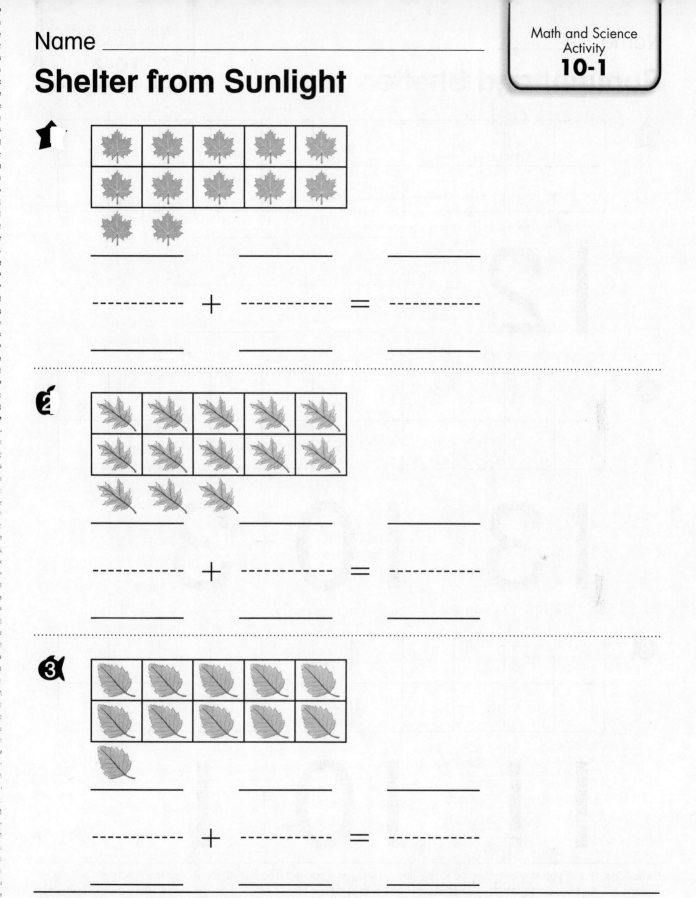

1

_____   _____   _____

---------- + ---------- = ----------

_____   _____   _____

2

_____   _____

---------- + ---------- = ----------

_____   _____   _____

3

_____   _____

---------- + ---------- = ----------

_____   _____   _____

Directions Say: _Did you know that plants in the rainforest shelter people, animals, and other plants from sunlight? Plants in the top layer of the rainforest must be tough in order to absorb a lot of sunlight. Most other plants would wilt or die if they were not protected from the heat coming from the sun._ **1**–**3** Have students write an equation to match the number of leaves shown. Then have them tell how the picture and equation show 10 ones and some more ones. **Extension** Have students draw 12 objects to show 10 ones and some more ones. Then have them explain the picture they drew.

Name _____

Sunlight and Shelter

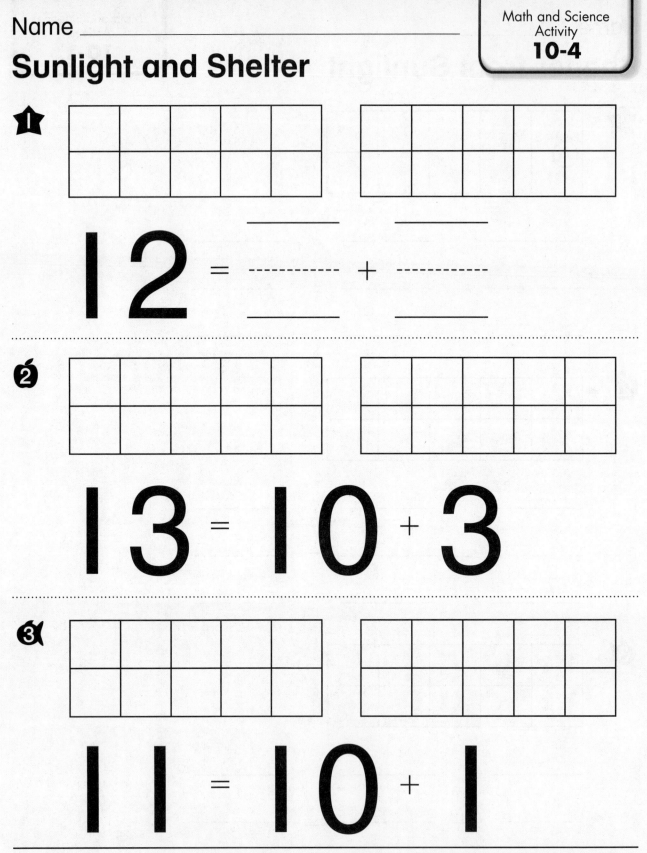

Directions Say: *If you stay outside on a sunny day too long, you can get a painful sunburn. Too much sunlight can be harmful to your skin. On sunny days, people can find shelter under a tree or inside a house to keep from getting burned by the sun.* Have students: ⭐ use counters to show 12, draw houses in the double ten-frame, and complete the equation to match the picture. Then have them tell how the picture and equation show 10 ones and some more ones; 🍎 draw trees in the double ten-frame to match the equation; 🐟 draw suns in the double ten-frame to match the equation. Then have them tell how the picture and equation show 10 ones and some more ones. **Extension** Have students draw a picture to match the equation 13 = 10 + 3. Then have them explain how the picture shows 10 ones and some more ones.

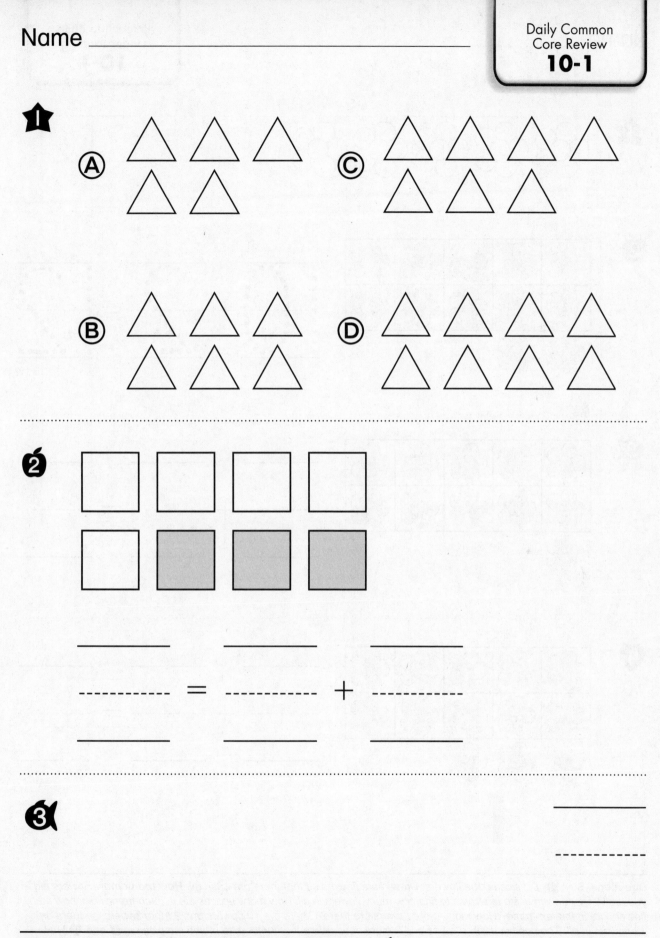

Directions Have students: mark the picture that shows 7 objects; ❷ write an equation that describes the picture; ❸ draw 11 eggs, and then write the number to tell how many.

1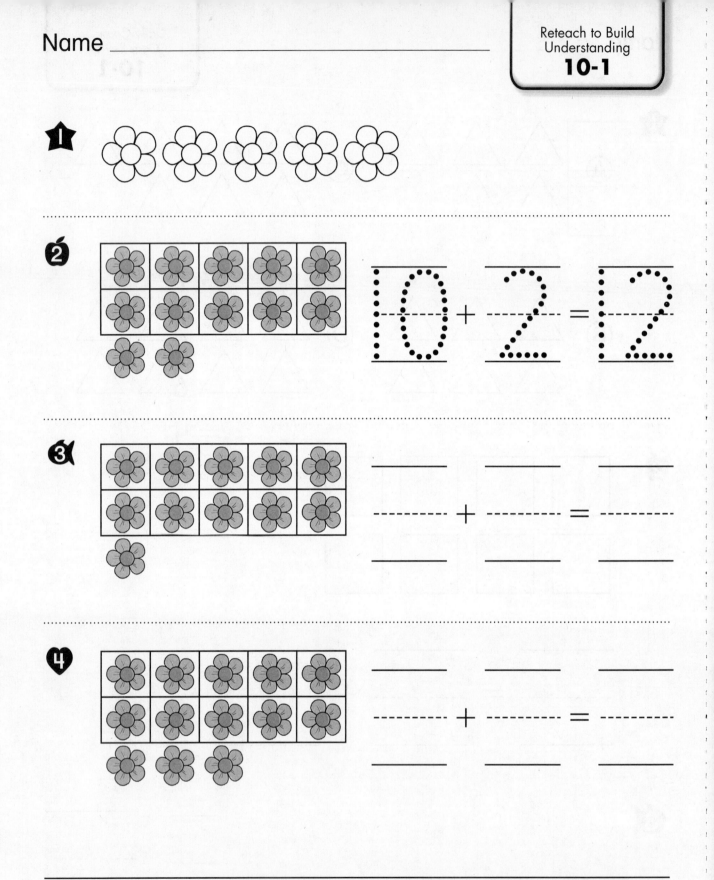

2 $10 + 2 = 12$

3 ___ + ___ = ___

4 ___ + ___ = ___

Directions Say: **1** *Let's count the flowers. Draw more flowers so that there are 10 in all.* **How many more** *flowers did you draw?* **2** *You can use a ten-frame to find how many flowers in all. How many spaces are in a ten-frame? So, how many flowers are in the ten-frame? How many more flowers are there? There are 10 flowers and 2 more flowers, so there are 12 flowers in all. The number 12 is 10 ones and 2 more ones. Write the numbers to match the picture.* **3** *and* **4** *Have students write an equation to match the number of flowers shown. Then have them tell how the picture and equation show 10 ones and some more ones.* **On the Back!** *Have students draw a picture to match the equation* 10 + 3 = 13.

 R 10·1

1

(A) $10 = 5 + 5$ (C) $10 = 7 + 3$

    $10 = 8 + 2$ $10 = 3 + 7$

(B) $9 = 5 + 4$ (D) $10 = 6 + 4$

    $9 = 4 + 5$ $10 = 4 + 6$

2

_____

- - - - - - - - - - -

_____

3

1	2	3	4	5	6	7	8	9	10
11	12	13	14	15	16	17	18	19	20

16

_____ _____ _____

- - - - - - - - - - - - - - - - - - - - - - - - - - - - - - - - -

_____ _____ _____

Directions Have students: **1** mark the set of equations that describes the picture; **2** count the counters, and then write the number that tells how many; **3** find the highlighted number on the number chart, count forward until they reach the stop sign, and then write each number they counted.

⭐

_____
- - - - - - - - - -
_____

🍎 $10 + 5 = 15$

⭐

_____ _____ _____

- - - - - - + - - - - - = - - - - -

_____ _____ _____

4

_____ _____ _____

- - - - - - + - - - - - = - - - - -

_____ _____ _____

Directions ⭐ Have students **count** the dogs, and then write the number that tells how many. 🍎 Say: *You can write an equation to match the counters in the ten-frames. Let's count the counters in the top ten-frame. Write that number. Count the counters in the bottom ten-frame. Write that number. How many counters are there in all? Complete the equation to match the picture. Your picture and equation show one way to make 15 with 10 ones and 5 more ones.* ⭐–4 Have students write an equation to match the counters. Then have them tell how the picture and equation show 10 ones and some more ones. **On the Back!** Have students draw counters to match the equation $10 + 5 = 15$.

1

10 + 5 = -----------

Ⓐ 16   Ⓒ 10
Ⓑ 15   Ⓓ 5

2

_____

- -

_____

3

Name _____

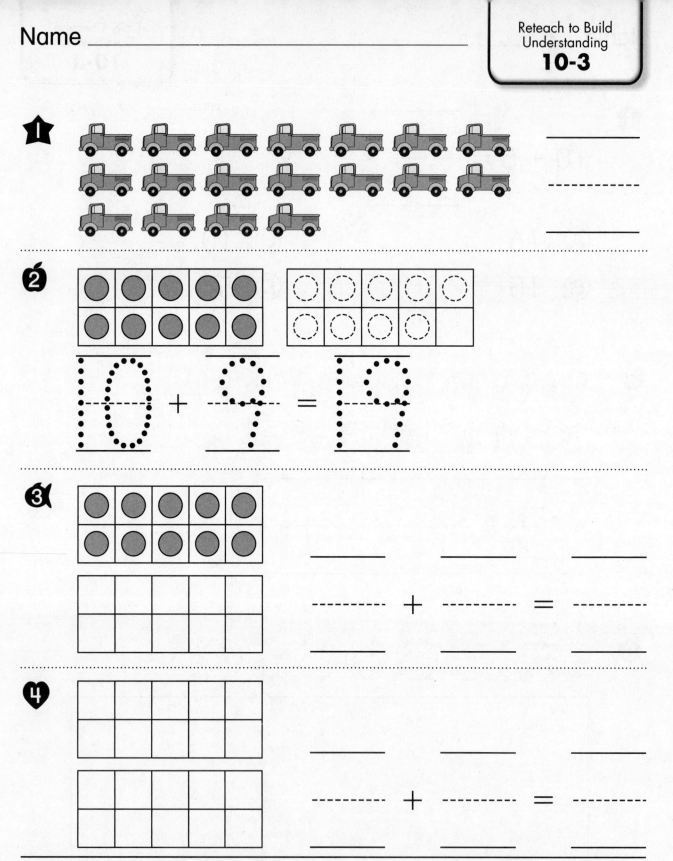

★ _____

_ _ _ _ _ _ _ _ _ _

_____

🍎 $10 + 9 = 19$

③ ___ ___ ___

_ _ _ _ _ _ + _ _ _ _ _ _ = _ _ _ _ _ _

④ ___ ___ ___

_ _ _ _ _ _ + _ _ _ _ _ _ = _ _ _ _ _ _

Directions ★ Have students **count** the trucks and then write the number that tells how many. 🍎 Say: *How many counters are in the first ten-frame? Draw more counters in the second ten-frame to show how to make 19. How many counters did you draw? Now write an equation to match the picture. The picture and equation show one way to make 19 with 10 ones and some more ones.* Have students draw counters, and then write an equation to: ③ show how to make 18. Then have them tell how the picture and equation show 10 ones and some more ones; ④ show how to make 17. Then have them tell how the picture and equation show 10 ones and some more ones. **On the Back!** Have students draw counters to match the equation $10 + 8 = 18$.

⭐ **1**

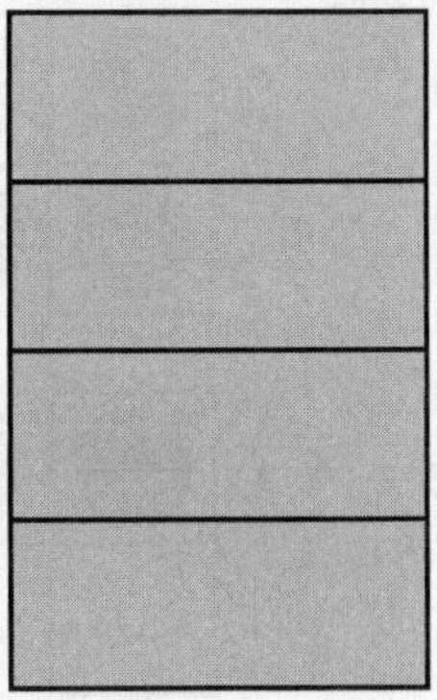

Ⓐ

Ⓑ

Ⓒ

Ⓓ

🍎 **2**

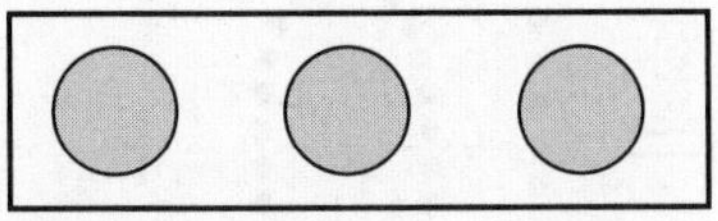

Ⓐ

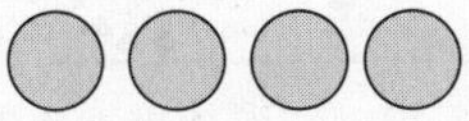

Ⓑ

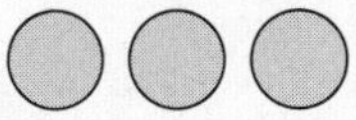

Ⓒ

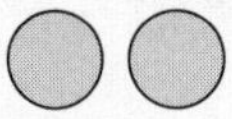

Ⓓ

3

_____

- - - - - - - - - - - - - - - - -

_____

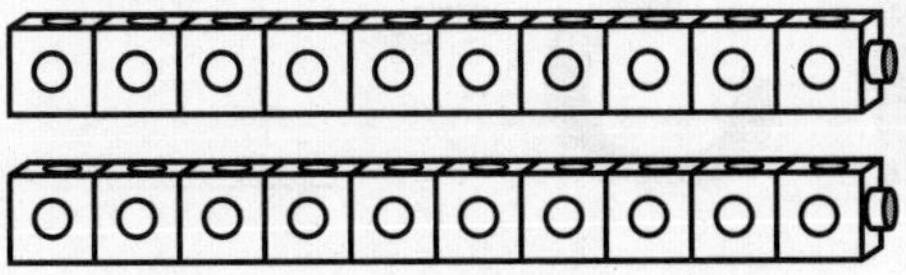

Directions Have students: ⭐ mark the picture that matches the number of shaded parts; 🍎 mark the group of counters that shows 1 fewer counter than the group of counters shown; **3** count the cubes, and then practice writing the number that tells how many.

D 10•4

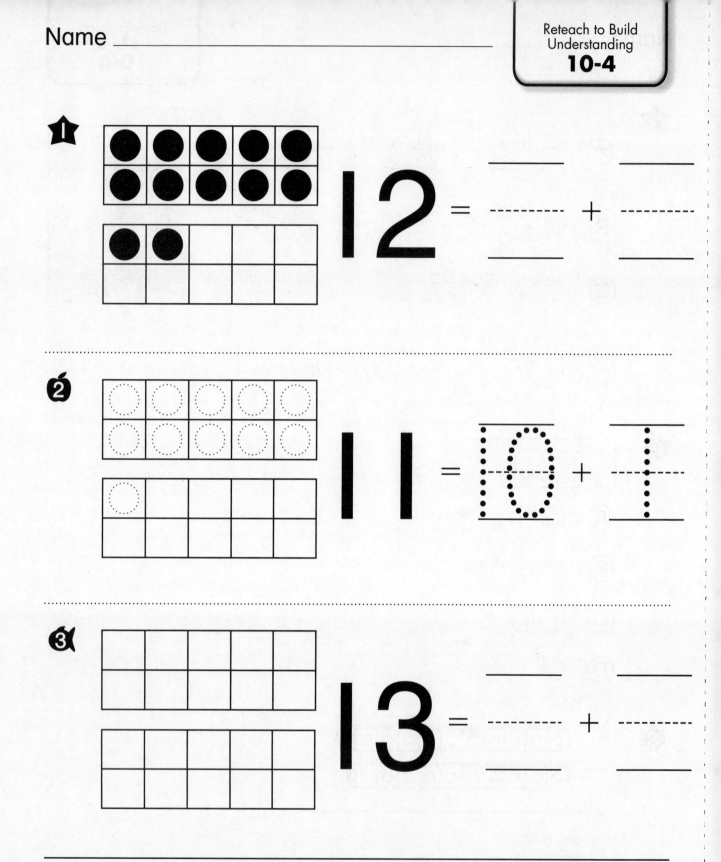

1

$12 = $ ___ + ___

2

$11 = 10 + 1$

3

$13 = $ ___ + ___

Directions ★ Have students write an **equation** to match the counters shown. Then have them tell how the picture and equation show 10 ones and some more ones. Have students use counters: **2** to show 11. Then say: *Draw counters in the double ten-frame to show 11. How many counters should you draw in the first ten-frame? How many in the second ten-frame? Write an equation to match the picture. Then tell how the picture and equation show 10 ones and some more ones.* **3** to show 13, draw them in the double ten-frame, and complete the equation to match the picture. Then have them tell how the picture and equation show 10 ones and some more ones. **On the Back!** Have students draw counters to match the equation $12 = 10 + 2$.

Name _____

1.

(A) 🌢🌢🌢🌢🌢

(B) 🌢🌢🌢🌢🌢🌢

(C) 🌢🌢🌢🌢🌢🌢🌢

(D) 🌢🌢🌢🌢🌢🌢🌢🌢

---

2. 3, 4, ____, 6

(A) 7   (C) 2

(B) 5   (D) 1

3.

____

- - - - - - - - - -

____

Directions Have students: **1** mark the picture that shows 7 raindrops; **2** mark the missing number; **3** count the animals, and then write the number that tells how many animals in all.

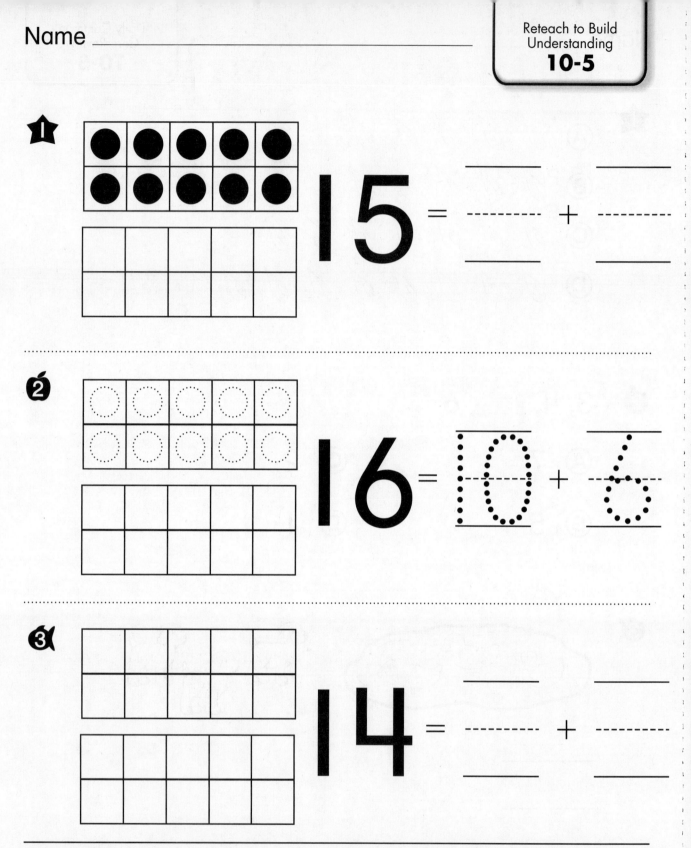

⭐

$15 =$ ____ + ____

🍎

$16 = 10 + 6$

⭐

$14 =$ ____ + ____

Directions ⭐ Say: *How many counters are in the first ten-frame?* **How many more** *counters should you draw in the second ten-frame to make 15? Draw that many counters, and then complete the equation to match the picture.* Have students use counters: 🍎 *to show 16.* Then say: *Draw counters in the double ten-frame to show 16. How many counters should you draw in the first ten-frame? How many in the second ten-frame? Complete the equation to match the picture. How does the picture and equation show 10 ones and some more ones?* ⭐ *to show 14, draw them in the double ten-frame, and complete the equation to match the picture.* Then have them tell how the picture and equation show 10 ones and some more ones. **On the Back!** Have students draw a picture to match the equation $15 = 10 + 5$. Then have them tell how the picture shows 10 ones and some more ones.

Listen and Learn

Start Put 4 5 and 6 in a .
Get 6 blue squares.

Mount Eagle School

Say 10 and ☐ more is _____.

Material Number tiles 4–6, a bag for the tiles, 6 blue squares

Oral Directions **TRY** Pick a number tile from the bag. Put your number tile in the first space of the sentence. Pretend the blue squares are books, and use that many blue squares to make a group of books. Ask your partner to count all the books on the page, and then say, "10 and ___ [5] more is ___ [15]." Count the books, and then say the sentence too. Set the tile aside. Take turns and play until the bag is empty.

TRY AGAIN If you have time, remove the squares. Put the tiles back in the bag. Play again!

Center Game ★ 10-5   K

Listen and Learn

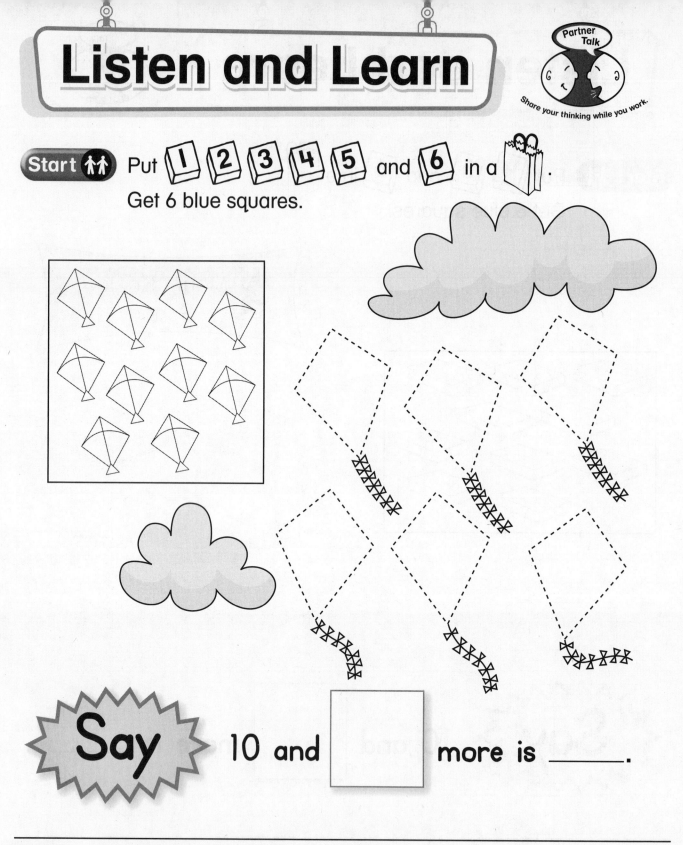

Partner Talk
Share your thinking while you work.

Start 👫 Put 1 2 3 4 5 and 6 in a 🛍.
Get 6 blue squares.

Say 10 and [ ] more is _____.

Materials	Number tiles 1–6, a bag for the tiles, 6 blue squares
Oral Directions	**TRY** Pick a number tile from the bag. Put that number tile in the first space of the sentence. Pretend the blue squares are kites. Ask your partner to use blue squares to show the number of kites on the tile. Count all of the kites on the page. Then say, "10 and ___ [3] more is ___ [13]." Let your partner count the kites. Ask your partner to say the sentence too. Set the tile aside. Take turns and play until the bag is empty.
	TRY AGAIN If you have time, remove the squares. Put the tiles back in the bag. Play again!

Center Game ★★ **10·5**

1

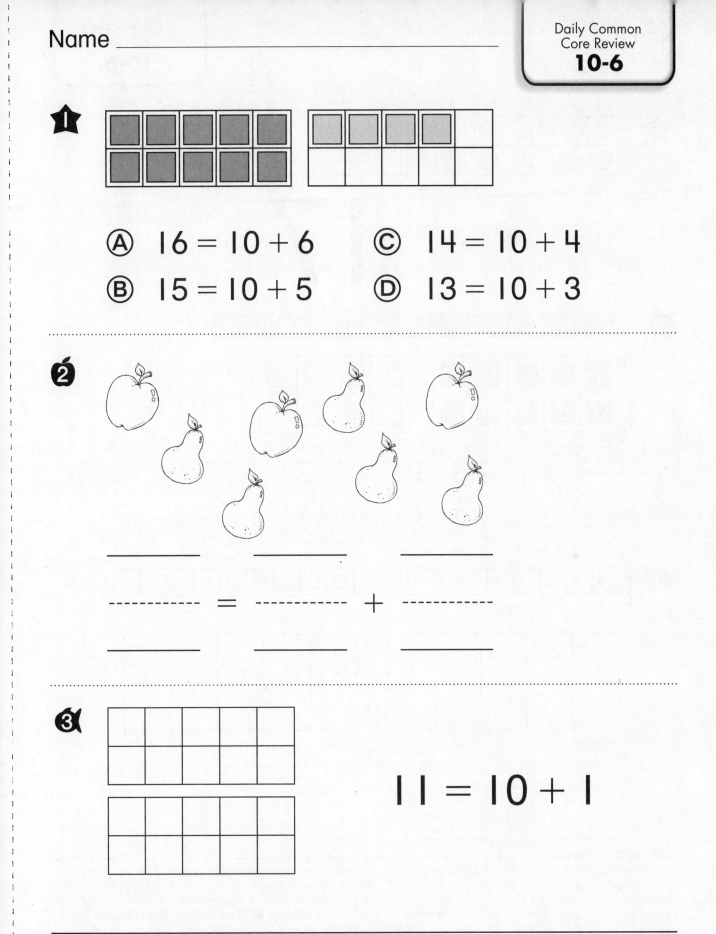

(A) $16 = 10 + 6$ (C) $14 = 10 + 4$

(B) $15 = 10 + 5$ (D) $13 = 10 + 3$

2

_____   _____   _____

- - - - - - = - - - - - - + - - - - - -

_____   _____   _____

3

$11 = 10 + 1$

Directions Have students: **1** mark the equation that matches the squares in the double ten-frame; **2** write an equation that describes the pieces of fruit; **3** draw counters to match the equation.

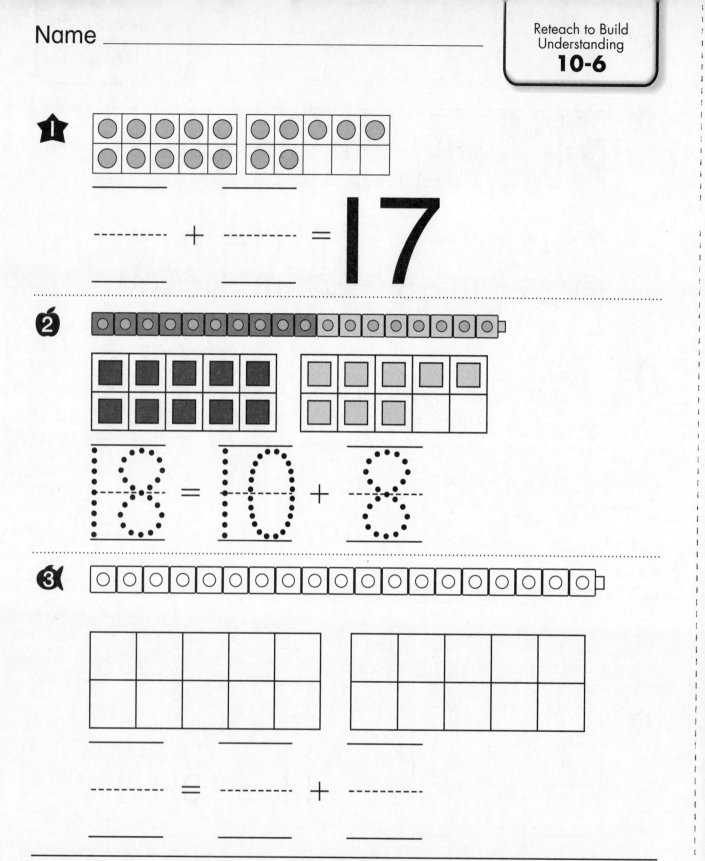

⭐ 1

_____ + _____ = **17**
_____   _____

🍎 2

18 = 10 + 8

⭐ 3

_____ = _____ + _____
_____   _____   _____

Directions Say: ⭐ *The double ten-frame shows 17. 17 is 10 and* **how many more** *ones? Complete the equation to match the picture;* 🍎 *Let's use the cube train to show 18. 18 is 10 ones and 8 more ones. Color 10 cubes blue. Color 8 cubes red. This shows one way to show 18. Now let's use the ten-frame to show 18. How many squares should you color blue? How many should you color red? Write an equation to match the pictures.* ⭐ Have students color 10 cubes blue to show 10 ones, and then draw 10 blue squares in the first ten-frame. Have them color the remaining cubes in the cube train red to show more ones, count them, and then draw red squares in the other ten-frame. Then have them write an equation to match the pictures. **On the Back!** Have students draw pictures to match the equation 17 = 10 + 7.

Look and See

Start 👫 Get 18 red squares. Get 🎲🎲🎲.

Materials	18 red squares, 3 dot cubes
Oral Directions	**TRY** Take turns. Toss 3 dot cubes. Count the dots. Say the number in all. Pretend your squares are fish. Show that number of fish in the fish tanks. Tell your partner if there are more fish in the top fish tank or in the bottom fish tank. Remove the squares. Take turns until each player gets 5 turns.
	TRY AGAIN If you have more time, play again!

Look and See

Start 👥 Put 0 1 2 3 4 5 6 7 8 and 9 in a 🛍.

Get 19 red squares.
Get 19 blue squares.

Materials 19 red squares, 19 blue squares, number tiles 0–9, paper bag

Oral Directions

TRY Decide who will fill the top fish tanks and who will fill the bottom fish tanks. Pretend your squares are fish. Take turns picking a tile and putting it next to the number 1 by your fish tank. For example, if you pick a 2, your number is 12. Say your number aloud. Use red and blue squares to show that number of fish in your tank. Compare the number of fish you have with your partner to see who has more fish. Set the tiles aside. Play until the bag is empty.

TRY AGAIN If you have more time, put the tiles back in the bag. Play again!

Center Game ★★ 10·6

⭐ 1

(A) $10 = 6 + 4$
$10 = 4 + 6$

(C) $6 = 4 + 2$
$6 = 2 + 4$

(B) $10 = 7 + 3$
$10 = 5 + 5$

(D) $10 = 2 + 8$
$10 = 8 + 2$

🍎 2

🍎 3

_____

- - - - - - - - - - -

_____

Directions ⭐ Have students mark the set of equations that describes the picture; 🍎 Say: *The animals have been classified into two categories. Mark all the animals that belong in the category of animals outside of the circle.* 🍎 Have students count the counters, and then write the number that tells how many.

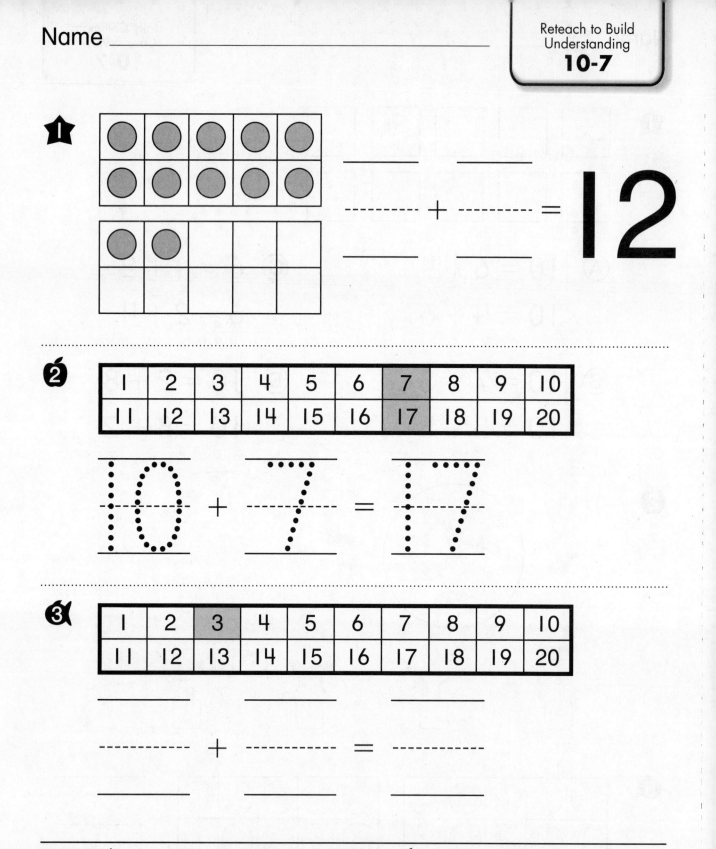

1

_____ _____ _____

_ _ _ _ _ _ + _ _ _ _ _ _ = 12

_____ _____

2

1	2	3	4	5	6	7	8	9	10
11	12	13	14	15	16	17	18	19	20

10 + 7 = 17

3

1	2	3	4	5	6	7	8	9	10
11	12	13	14	15	16	17	18	19	20

_____ _____ _____

_ _ _ _ _ _ + _ _ _ _ _ = _ _ _ _ _

_____ _____ _____

Directions ⭐ Have students write an **equation** to match the picture. ❷ Point to the highlighted number in the top row. Say: *How can you use this chart to find the number that is 10 greater than 7? Let's count forward 10 together.* Point to each number as you count and stop at 17. *What number is 10 greater? Color that number.* Have students write an equation to match, and then tell how the equation shows 10 ones and some more ones. Describe the pattern. ❸ Have students find the highlighted number, and then color the number that is 10 greater than the highlighted number. Have them write an equation to match, and then tell how the equation shows 10 ones and some more ones. Then have students explain the pattern they made. **On the Back!** Have students draw pictures to match the equation 11 = 10 + 1. Then have them tell how the picture shows 10 ones and some more ones.

Play a Game

Start 👥 Get 18 red squares. Get 10 blue squares.

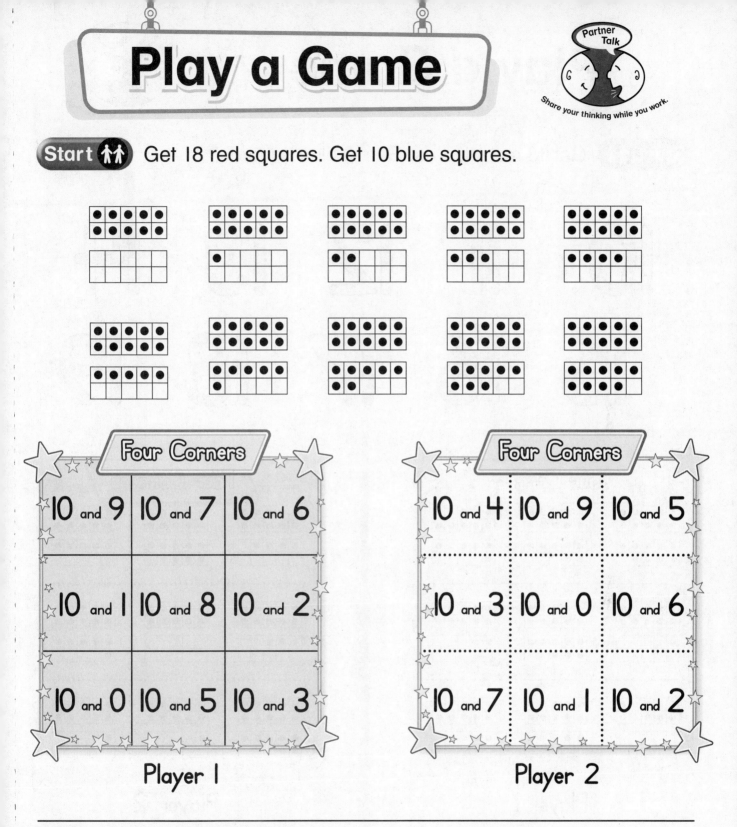

Four Corners

10 and 9	10 and 7	10 and 6
10 and 1	10 and 8	10 and 2
10 and 0	10 and 5	10 and 3

Player 1

Four Corners

10 and 4	10 and 9	10 and 5
10 and 3	10 and 0	10 and 6
10 and 7	10 and 1	10 and 2

Player 2

Materials   18 red squares, 10 blue squares

Oral Directions   **TRY** Use 10 blue squares to cover the pictures above the game boards. Decide who will be Player 1 and who will be Player 2. Find your game board. Get 9 red squares for each player. Take turns. Uncover a picture. Tell your partner how many counters are in the double ten-frame. For example, say, "I see 10 and 6 more. There are 16 counters." Any player who has that number in a game space covers it. The first player to cover all 4 corners wins.

TRY AGAIN If you have more time, play again!

Play a Game

Start 👥 Get 18 red squares. Get 10 blue squares.

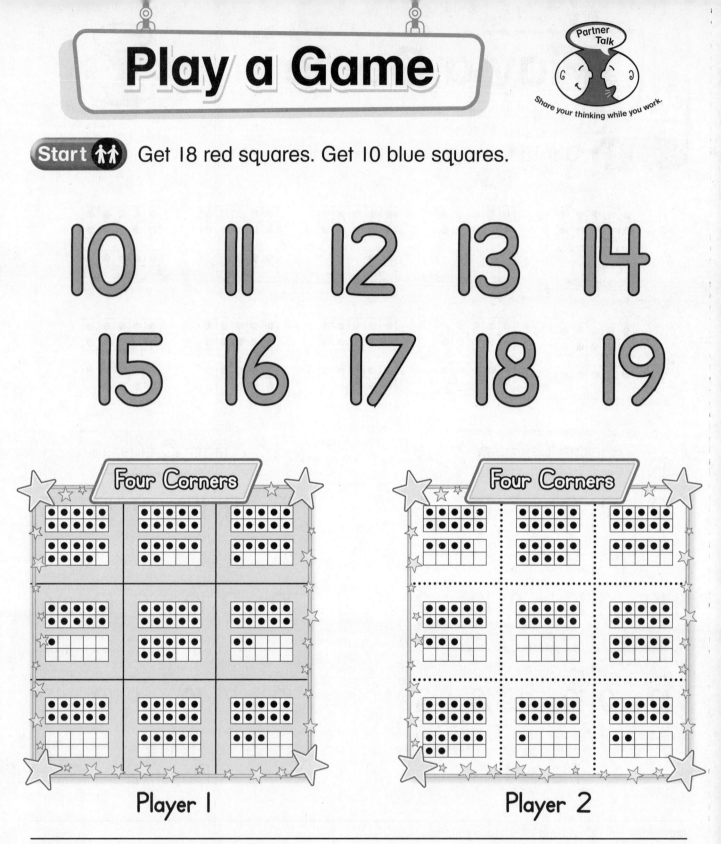

10 11 12 13 14
15 16 17 18 19

Four Corners

Player 1

Four Corners

Player 2

Materials	18 red squares, 10 blue squares
Oral Directions	**TRY** Cover each number above the game boards with a blue square. Decide who will be Player 1 and who will be Player 2. Find your game board. Get 9 red squares for each player. Take turns. Uncover a number. Say that number. Any player who has a game space with the double ten-frame that shows that number covers the game space. The first player to cover all 4 corners wins.
	TRY AGAIN If you have more time, play again!

This book belongs to:

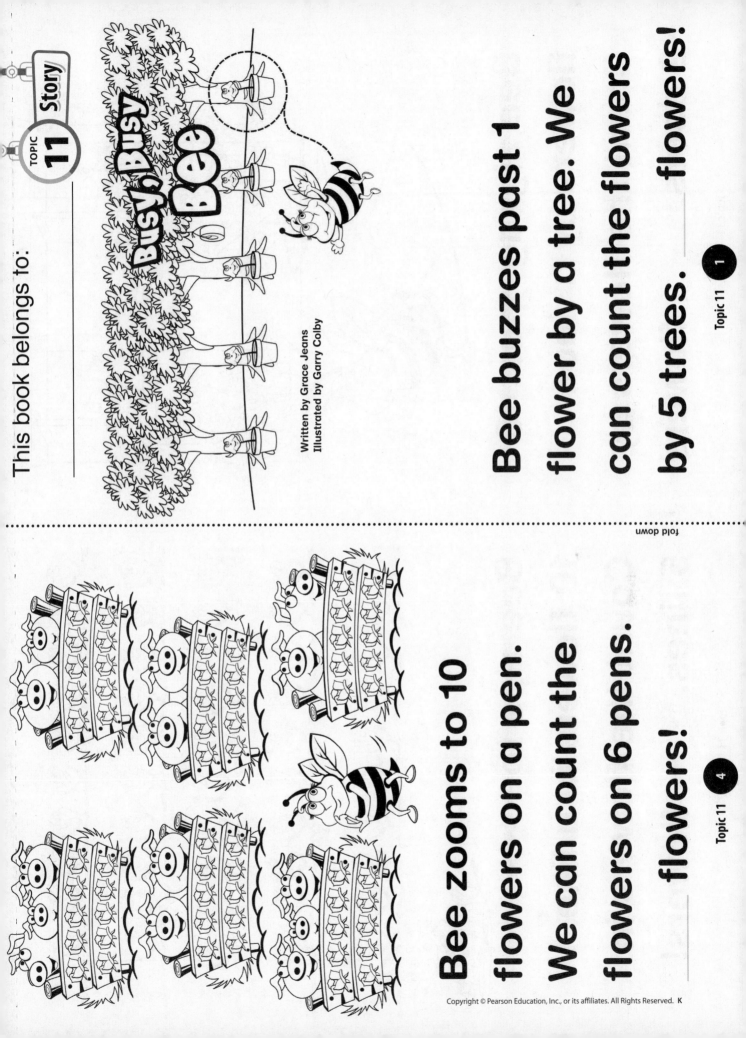

Busy, Busy
Bee

Written by Grace Jeans
Illustrated by Garry Colby

fold down

Bee buzzes past 1 flower by a tree. We can count the flowers by 5 trees. _____ flowers!

Topic 11   **1**

Bee zooms to 10 flowers on a pen. We can count the flowers on 6 pens. _____ flowers!

Topic 11   **4**

Bee zigzags past 10
flowers by a door.
Count the flowers by
2 doors. _____ flowers!

fold up

Bee zips to
10 flowers in a line.
Count the flowers in
5 lines. _____ flowers!

Name _____

Count Numbers to 100

Topic 11 Standards
K.CC.A.1, K.CC.A.2
See the front of the Student's Edition for complete standards.

Dear Family,

Your child is learning to work with larger numbers through 100. In this topic, he or she will learn to count and read numbers to 100. Your child will also learn to use a hundred chart to recognize patterns when counting by tens and ones.

Numbers on a Hundred Chart
Numbers are counted and written in a specific sequence on a hundred chart.
Use a hundred chart to count to 100.

1	2	3	4	5	6	7	8	9	10
11	12	13	14	15	16	17	18	19	20
21	22	23	24	25	26	27	28	29	30
31	32	33	34	35	36	37	38	39	40
41	42	43	44	45	46	47	48	49	50
51	52	53	54	55	56	57	58	59	60
61	62	63	64	65	66	67	68	69	70
71	72	73	74	75	76	77	78	79	80
81	82	83	84	85	86	87	88	89	90
91	92	93	94	95	96	97	98	99	100

Try this activity with your child to practice using a hundred chart.

Guess the Number

Play "Guess the Number." Say, "I am thinking of a number that comes just after 91. What number is it?" Encourage your child to use the chart to find the correct number, and then say the number aloud. You may wish to write each number that your child finds.

Observe Your Child

Focus on Mathematical Practice 5:
Use appropriate tools strategically.

Help your child become proficient with Mathematical Practice 5. Using the hundred chart, point to a number in the top row and have your child count by 10s from that number. Ask your child to color the pattern, and then explain how he or she knows the pattern is right.

Contar números hasta 100

Estándares del Tema 11

K.CNC.A.1, K.CNC.A.2

Los estándares completos se encuentran en las páginas preliminares del
Libro del estudiante.

Estimada familia:

Su niño(a) está aprendiendo a trabajar con números más grandes hasta el 100. En este tema, él o ella aprenderá a contar y leer números hasta 100. Su niño(a) también aprenderá a usar una tabla de 100 para reconocer patrones cuando cuente decenas y unidades.

Números en una tabla de 100

En una tabla de 100, los números se cuentan y escriben en una secuencia específica. Use una tabla de 100 para contar hasta 100.

1	2	3	4	5	6	7	8	9	10
11	12	13	14	15	16	17	18	19	20
21	22	23	24	25	26	27	28	29	30
31	32	33	34	35	36	37	38	39	40
41	42	43	44	45	46	47	48	49	50
51	52	53	54	55	56	57	58	59	60
61	62	63	64	65	66	67	68	69	70
71	72	73	74	75	76	77	78	79	80
81	82	83	84	85	86	87	88	89	90
91	92	93	94	95	96	97	98	99	100

Intente esta actividad con su niño(a) para practicar el uso de una tabla de 100.

Adivinar el número

Jueguen "Adivinar el número". Diga: "Estoy pensando en un número que va justo después de 91. ¿Qué número es?" Anime a su niño(a) a usar la tabla para hallar el número correcto y a decir el número en voz alta. Quizá quiera escribir cada número que halle su niño(a).

Observe a su niño(a)

Enfoque en la Práctica matemática 5:

Utilizar herramientas apropiadas de manera estratégica.

Ayude a su niño(a) a adquirir competencia en la Práctica matemática 5. Usando la tabla de 100, señale un número de la fila de arriba y pídale a su niño(a) que cuente de 10 en 10 a partir de ese número. Pídale que coloree el patrón y que luego explique cómo sabe que el patrón es correcto.

Bees

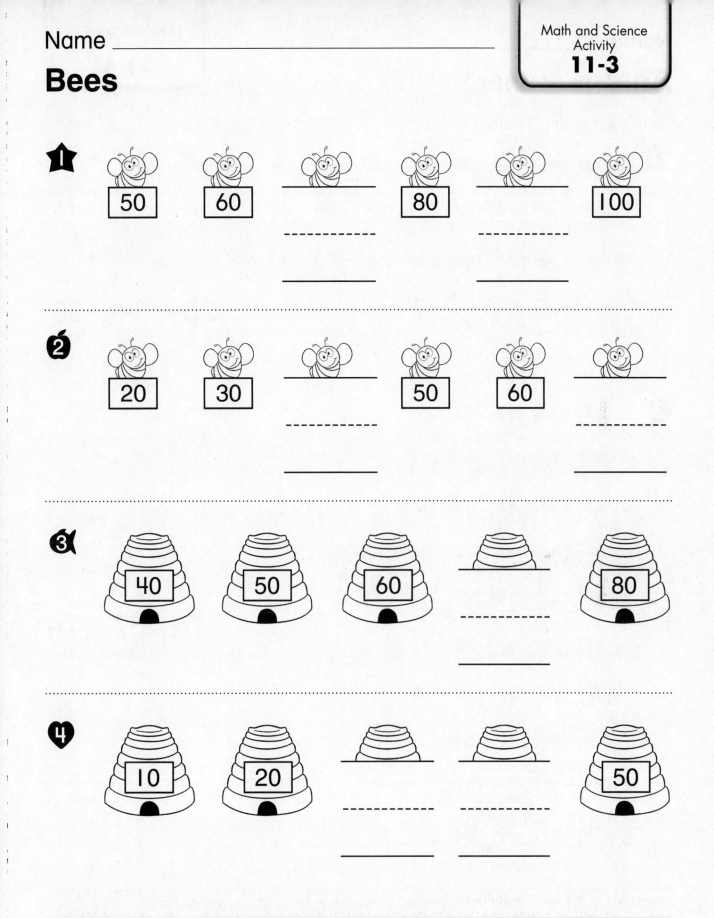

1 50   60   ____   80   ____   100

2 20   30   ____   50   60   ____

3 40   50   60   ____   80

4 10   20   ____   ____   50

Directions Say: *Did you know that bees live in colonies just like ants? Their home is called a hive.* **1**–**4** Have students write the missing numbers to complete the pattern. **Extension** Have students draw a row of 5 objects. Have them write the number 20 under the first object, and then continue to count up by tens, writing the numbers under each object.

Name _____

Ants

①

25   34   35

②

47   57   74

Directions Say: *Did you know ants are social insects and live in large groups? A group of ants is called a colony.*
Have students: ① count the rows of ants by tens and by ones, and then draw a circle around the number that tells how many; ② count the columns of ants by tens and by ones, and then draw a circle around the number that tells how many.
Extension Have students draw a colony of 56 ants. They can draw circles to represent the ants if they choose. Have them draw 5 rows of 10 ants, and a row of 6 ants.

Math and Science Activity 11·4   Copyright © Pearson Education, Inc., or its affiliates. All Rights Reserved. K

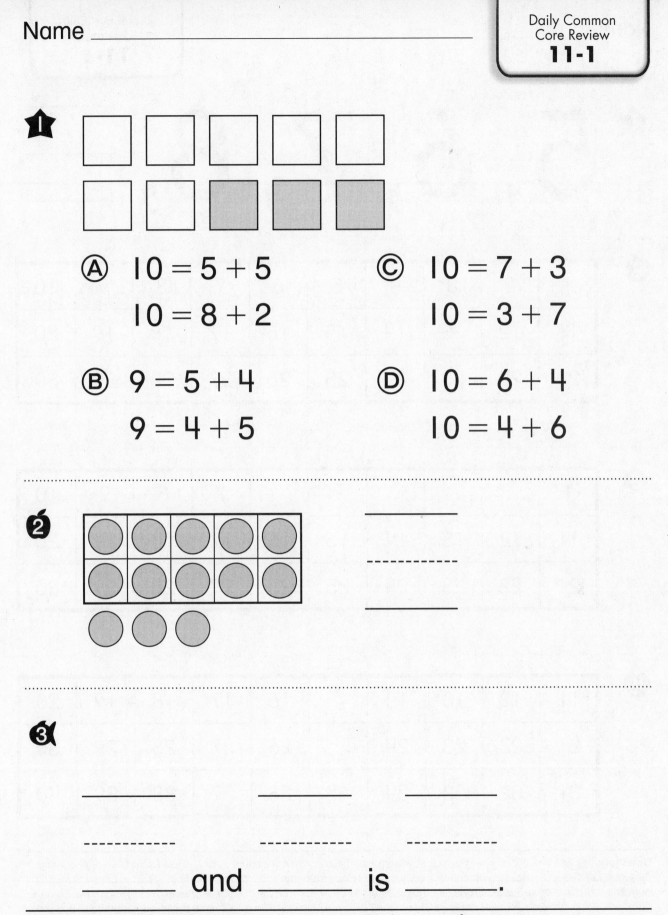

⭐ 1

Ⓐ $10 = 5 + 5$
$10 = 8 + 2$

Ⓒ $10 = 7 + 3$
$10 = 3 + 7$

Ⓑ $9 = 5 + 4$
$9 = 4 + 5$

Ⓓ $10 = 6 + 4$
$10 = 4 + 6$

🍎 2

_____

_____

⭐ 3

_____   _____   _____
-----------   -----------   -----------
_____ and _____ is _____.

Directions Have students: ⭐1 mark the set of equations that matches the picture; 🍎2 count the counters, and then write the number that tells how many; ⭐3 draw two groups of animals to show 9 in all, and then write a number sentence to match the drawing.

D 11·1

⭐ 5, 6, 7, 8, ____ ____

1	2	3	4	5	6	7	8	9	10
11	12	13	14	15	16	17	18	19	20
21	22	23	24	25	26	27	28	29	30

❸

1						7	8	9	10
11	12	13	14	15	16	17	18	19	20
21	22	23	24	25	26	27	28	29	30

❹

11	12	13	14		16	17	18	19	20
21	22	23	24		26	27	28	29	30
31	32	33	34		36	37	38	39	40

Directions ⭐ Point to the numbers as you say them aloud. Say: *When we count 5, 6, 7, 8, and so on, we are counting by **ones**. Let's keep counting. What number comes next?* Have students write the next number. ❷ Say: *Listen to these numbers, and then draw a circle around the numbers in the chart that you hear: eight, eighteen, twenty-eight. How are the numbers with a circle around them alike? How are they different?* Have students: ❸ write the missing numbers, and then explain how they know the numbers are correct; ❹ write the missing numbers, say them aloud, and then explain how the numbers in that column are alike. **On the Back!** Have students write the numbers 15, 16, 17, and 18. Then have them write the next four numbers.

R 11·1

1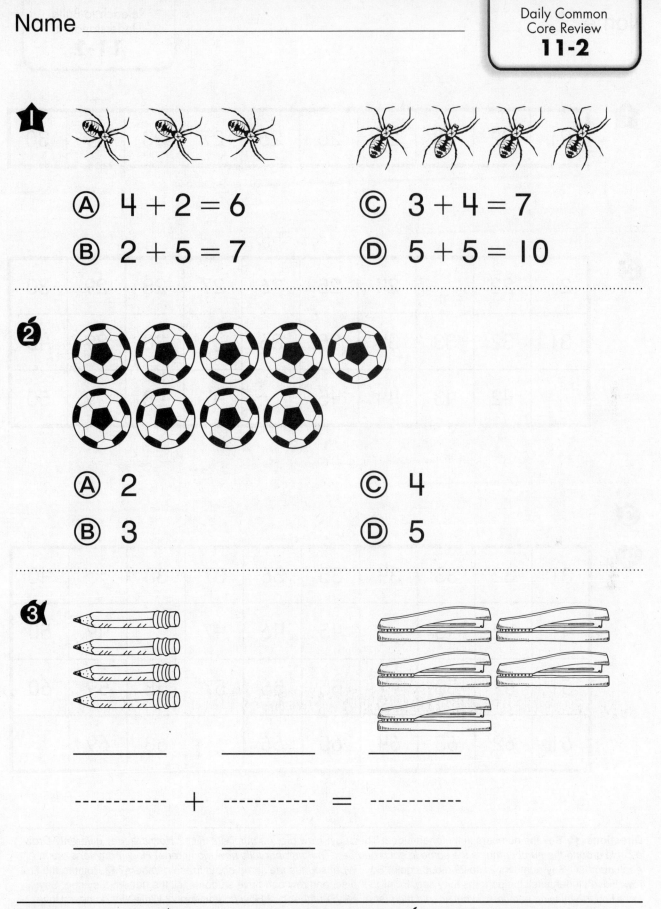

Ⓐ $4 + 2 = 6$ Ⓒ $3 + 4 = 7$

Ⓑ $2 + 5 = 7$ Ⓓ $5 + 5 = 10$

2

Ⓐ 2   Ⓒ 4

Ⓑ 3   Ⓓ 5

3

_____   _____   _____

---------- + ---------- = ----------

_____   _____   _____

Directions Have students: **1** mark the equation that matches the picture; **2** listen to the story, and then mark the number that tells how many soccer balls are left. Say: *Mrs. Carter has 9 soccer balls in her school office. She gives 5 balls to Mr. Young. How many soccer balls does Mrs. Carter have left?* **3** write an equation that matches the picture.

⭐ **1**

21	22	23	24	25	26	27	28	29	30

2

21	22	23	24	25	26	27	28	29	30
31	32	33	34	35	36	37	38	39	40
41	42	43	44	45	46	47	48	49	50

3

4

31	32	33	34	35	36	37	38		40
41	42	43		45	46	47		49	50
51	52	53		55	56	57	58	59	60
61	62	63	64	65	66		68	69	

Directions ⭐ Say the numbers in the chart aloud. Then say: *How are the numbers alike? How are they different? Draw a circle around the number that is the same in each number. That number tells how many* **tens.** *How many tens are in each number? Say numbers 21 to 29 aloud again. Say: What sounds the same about these numbers?* **2** Point to the first row. Have students tell the patterns they see. Point to the second row and have students tell the pattern they see. Say: *Let's find the missing numbers. What should the first missing number be? How do you know? Write that number.* Have students continue to write the missing numbers. Have students: **3** write the missing numbers, and then explain how they found the numbers; **4** color the boxes of the numbers that have 4 in the tens place. **On the Back!** Have students write the numbers 25, 35, 45, and 55, and then draw a circle around the number in the tens place for each number.

R 11-2

Look and See

Partner Talk
Share your thinking while you work.

Start 👥 Put ⬜1⬜ 2 3 4 5 in a 🛍.

⬜ 0 eggs

Materials   Number tiles 1–5, a bag for the tiles

Oral Directions   **TRY** Take turns. Pick a tile. Count that number of chickens. Put the tile in the space at the bottom of the page. Count aloud by 10s to count the number of eggs those chickens have in all. Then ask your partner to count aloud by 10s to count the number of eggs those chickens have in all. Remove the tile. Take turns until the bag of tiles is empty.

TRY AGAIN If you have time, put the tiles back in the bag. Begin again!

Look and See

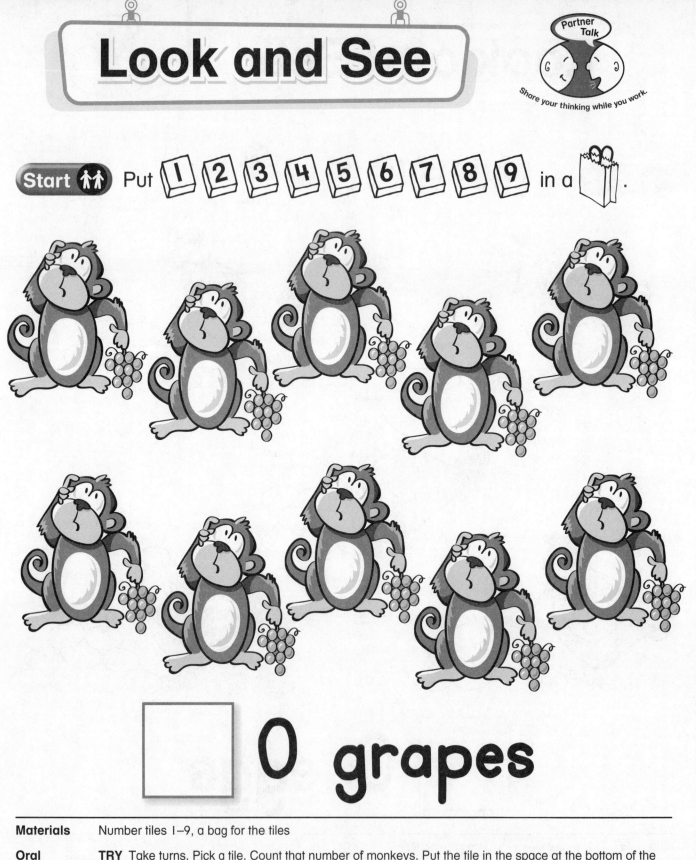

Start 👥 Put ① ② ③ ④ ⑤ ⑥ ⑦ ⑧ ⑨ in a 🛍.

☐ 0 grapes

Materials	Number tiles 1–9, a bag for the tiles
Oral Directions	**TRY** Take turns. Pick a tile. Count that number of monkeys. Put the tile in the space at the bottom of the page. Count aloud by 10s to count the number of grapes those monkeys have in all. Then ask your partner to count the grapes those monkeys have in all. Remove the tile. Take turns until the bag of tiles is empty.
	TRY AGAIN If you have time, tell how many grapes all of the monkeys have. Then take turns. Put a tile in the space at the bottom of the activity page. Ask your partner to tell how many monkeys have that number of grapes in all.

Center Game ★★ 11·2

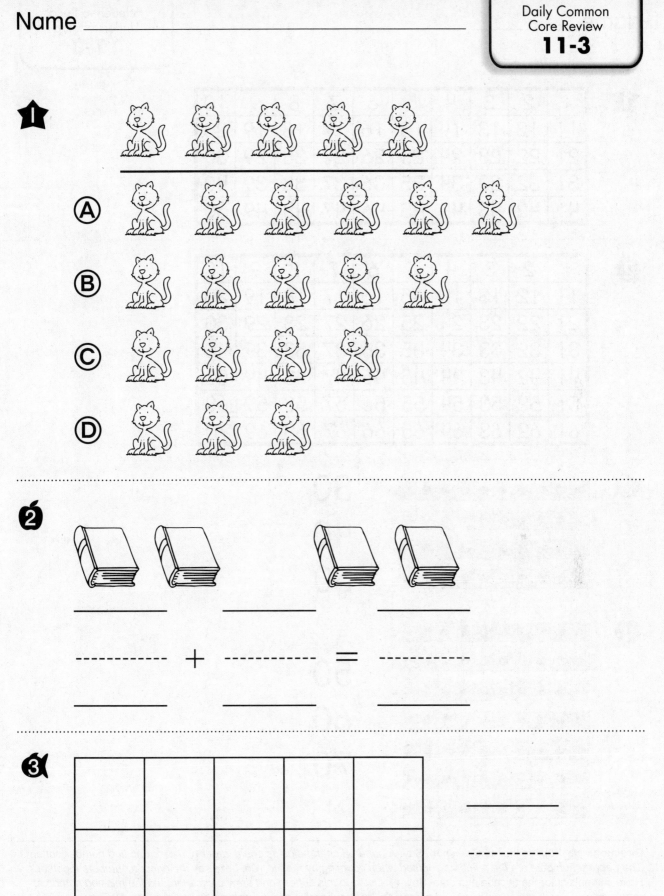

1

Ⓐ

Ⓑ

Ⓒ

Ⓓ

2

_____ _____

- - - - - - - - - - - + - - - - - - - - - - = - - - - - - - - - -

_____ _____ _____

3

_____

- - - - - - - - - -

_____

Directions Have students: **1** mark the group that shows 1 fewer cat than the group of cats at the top; **2** write an equation that tells about joining the two groups of books; **3** draw 9 counters, and then write the number that tells how many.

1

1	2	3	4	5	6	7	8	9	10
11	12	13	14	15	16	17	18	19	20
21	22	23	24	25	26	27	28	29	30
31	32	33	34	35	36	37	38	39	40
41	42	43	44	45	46	47	48	49	50

2

1	2	3	4	5	6	7	8	9	10
11	12	13	14	15	16	17	18	19	20
21	22	23	24	25	26	27	28	29	30
31	32	33	34	35	36	37	38	39	40
41	42	43	44	45	46	47	48	49	50
51	52	53	54	55	56	57	58	59	60
61	62	63	64	65	66	67	68	69	70

3

30

40

50

4

50

60

70

Directions ⭐ Point to the hundred chart. Say: *A hundred chart helps us count larger numbers and find number patterns. The* **decade** *numbers are the numbers counted when counting by tens to 100. Let's say the decade numbers together.* Have students color the decade numbers. Say: **2** *Listen to this pattern and draw a circle around the missing numbers: ten, twenty, _____, forty, _____, _____, seventy;* **3** *Each cube train has the same number of cubes. How many cubes are in the first cube train? Let's count by tens to find how many cubes in all. Draw a circle around that number.* **4** Have students count the cubes, and then draw a circle around the number that tells how many. **On the Back!** Have students write the decade numbers from 10 to 100.

R 11·3

Name _____

1 ⭐ $4 + 4 = 8$

(A)

(C)

(B)

(D)

2

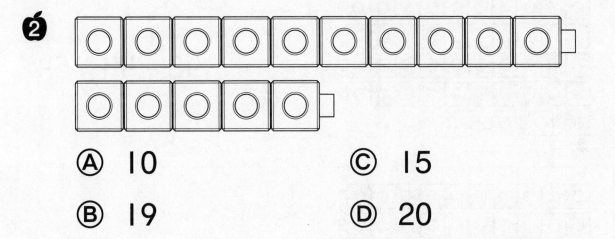

(A) 10   (C) 15

(B) 19   (D) 20

3

1	2	3	4	5	6	7	8	9	10
11	12	13	14	15	16	17	18	19	20
21	22	23	24	25	26	27	28	29	30
31	32	33	34	35	36	37	38	39	40
41	42	43	44	45	46	47	48	49	50

Directions Have students: ⭐ mark the picture that matches the equation; **2** mark the number that tells how many cubes; **3** draw a circle around each of the decade numbers.

Name _____

★1

20   30   40

🍎2

10
20
30
40
50

57   58   59

◆3

43   44   54

♥4

56   65   66

Directions Say: ★1 *How many cubes are in 1 cube train? How many* **rows** *of cubes are there? Count by tens to find how many in all. Draw a circle around the number that tells how many;* 🍎2 *Look at the picture. There are 5 cube trains and 7 loose cubes. You can count by tens and then by ones to find how many in all. There are 10 cubes in each cube train. Let's count the 5 cube trains by tens: 10, 20, 30, 40, 50. Now let's continue counting, and count the loose cubes by ones: 51, 52, 53, 54, 55, 56, 57. There are 57 cubes in all. Which number shows 5 tens and 7 ones? Draw a circle around that number.* ◆3 *and* ♥4 *Have students count by tens and by ones, and then draw a circle around the number that tells how many.* **On the Back!** *Using 40 or more small objects, have students count by tens and by ones to find how many in all, and then write the number that tells how many.*

R 11·4

1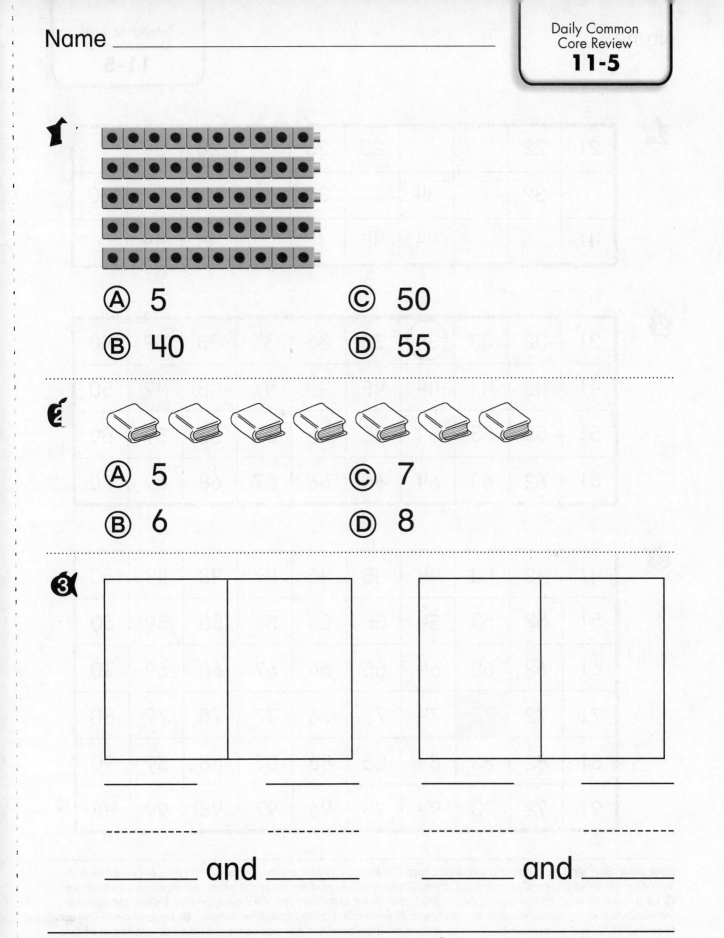

(A) 5   (C) 50

(B) 40   (D) 55

2

(A) 5   (C) 7

(B) 6   (D) 8

3

_____   _____   _____   _____

- - - - - - - - -   - - - - - - - - -   - - - - - - - - -   - - - - - - - - -

_____ and _____   _____ and _____

Directions Have students: **1** mark the number that tells how many cubes; **2** mark the number that tells how many books; **3** use counters, and then draw two different ways to make 10. Then have them write the numbers to tell the parts.

 D 11·5

★1

21	22			25	26		28	29	
	32		34		36				40
41			44	45			48	49	

②

31	32	33	(34)	35	36	37	38	39	40
41	42	43	44	45	46	47	48	49	50
51	52	53	54	55	56	57	58	59	60
61	62	63	64	65	66	67	68	69	70

③

41	42	43	44	45	46	47	48	49	50
51	52	53	54	55	56	57	58	59	60
61	62	63	64	65	66	67	68	69	70
71	72	73	74	75	76	77	78	79	80
81	82	83	84	85	86	87	88	89	90
91	92	93	94	95	96	97	98	99	100

Directions Say: ★ *This is part of a **hundred chart**. A hundred chart shows the numbers 1 to 100. Let's count by ones from 21 to 50. What two numbers come just after 22? Write those numbers. Write the other missing numbers as we count;* ② *Let's count some of the numbers in the hundred chart. Point to the number with a circle around it. Color the boxes of the numbers you say as you count aloud, starting at 34 and ending at the highlighted number.* ③ Have students find and draw a circle around the number 58. Then have them color the numbers they say as they count aloud, starting at 58 and ending at the highlighted number. **On the Back!** Have students write a number between 60 and 70. Then have them write the numbers they say as they count aloud, starting at the number they chose and ending at the number 95.

R 11·5

Look and See

Start 👫 Put 0 1 2 3 4 5 6 7 8 9 in a 🛍.

| Put your tile here. | Put your tile here. |

1	2	3	4	5	6	7	8	9	10
11	12	13	14	15	16	17	18	19	20
21	22	23	24	25	26	27	28	29	30
31	32	33	34	35	36	37	38	39	40
41	42	43	44	45	46	47	48	49	50
51	52	53	54	55	56	57	58	59	60
61	62	63	64	65	66	67	68	69	70
71	72	73	74	75	76	77	78	79	80
81	82	83	84	85	86	87	88	89	90
91	92	93	94	95	96	97	98	99	100

Materials Number tiles 0–9, a bag for the tiles

Oral Directions **TRY** Work with a partner. Pick 2 tiles. Put them in the empty spaces above the chart. Say the number you make. For example, say, "23." Point to that number on the hundred chart. Say the number that comes just before this number. Point to it. Ask your partner to point to and say the number that comes just after that number. Repeat until the bag is empty.

TRY AGAIN If you have time, play again! This time, count aloud to 100 from your number. As you count, point to each number in the hundred chart.

Look and See

Start 👥 Put 1 2 3 4 5 6 7 8 9

and 0 1 2 3 4 5 6 7 8 in a 🛍️.

Put your tile here.	Put your tile here.

1	2	3	4	5	6	7	8	9	10
11	12	13	14	15	16	17	18	19	20
21	22	23	24	25	26	27	28	29	30
31	32	33	34	35	36	37	38	39	40
41	42	43	44	45	46	47	48	49	50
51	52	53	54	55	56	57	58	59	60
61	62	63	64	65	66	67	68	69	70
71	72	73	74	75	76	77	78	79	80
81	82	83	84	85	86	87	88	89	90
91	92	93	94	95	96	97	98	99	100

Materials   Number tiles 1–9, number tiles 0–8, a bag for the tiles

Oral Directions   **TRY** Work with a partner. Pick 2 tiles. Put them in the empty spaces above the chart. Take turns. Say the number you make. For example, say, "53." Point to that number in the hundred chart. Say the two numbers that come just before that number. Point to them. Ask your partner to point to and say the two numbers that come just after that number. Change the order of the tiles and play again! If one of your tiles is 0, do not change the order of the tiles. Repeat until the bag of tiles is empty.

TRY AGAIN If you have time, play again! This time, count aloud to 100 from your number. As you count, point to each number in the hundred chart.

Center Game ★★ **11·5**

Name _____

⭐ **1**

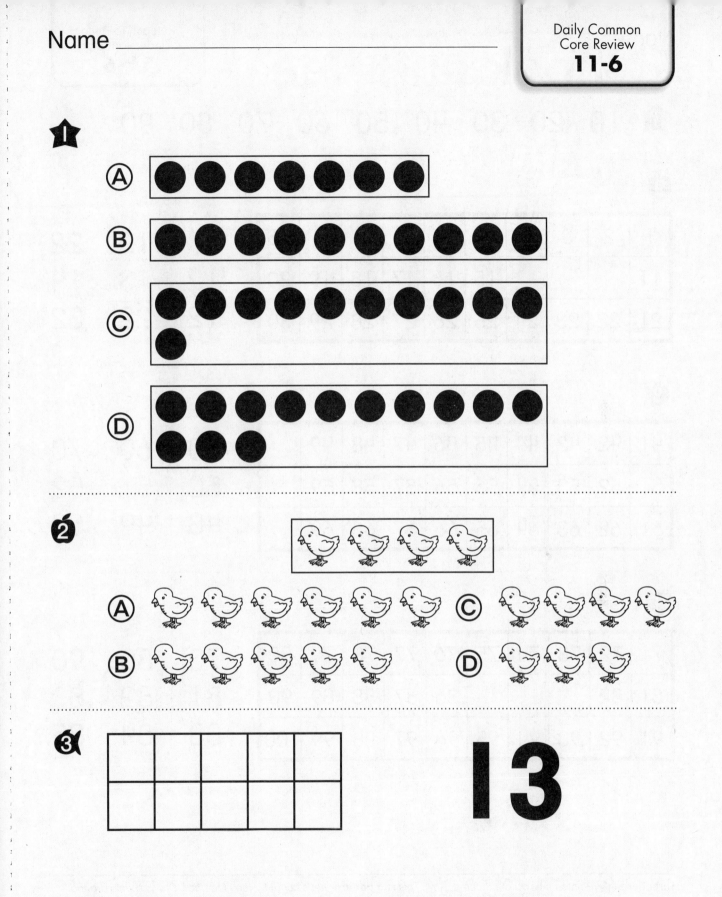

🍎 **2**

🐦 **3**

13

Directions Have students: ⭐ mark the picture that shows 7 counters; 🍎 mark the group of chicks that is less in number than the group of chicks in the box; 🐦 draw counters to show the number.

⭐ 10 20 30 40 50 60 70 80 90

②

1	2	3	4	5	6	7	8	9	10
11				15	16	17	18	19	20
21	22	23	24	25	26	27	28	29	30

2   12   22

12   13   14

12   22   32

③

41	42	43	44	45	46	47	48	49	
51	52	53	54	55	56	57	58	59	
61	62	63	64	65	66	67	68	69	

50   60   70

50   51   52

48   49   50

④

71	72	73	74	75	76	77	78	79	80
81	82				86	87	88	89	90
91	92	93	94	95	96	97	98	99	100

70   80   90

81   82   83

83   84   85

Directions ⭐ Point to the row of numbers. Say: *This is a* **pattern.** *Let's count by tens together. Draw a circle around each 0 that repeats in this pattern.* **②** Point to each number as you count aloud with students. Have them say the missing numbers as you count forward. Then have them draw a circle around the row that shows the missing set of numbers. **③** and **④** Have students count forward, and then draw a circle around the row that shows the missing set of numbers. **On the Back!** Have students draw a circle around a number between 1 and 20 on a hundred chart, count by tens from that number to the bottom of the chart, and then draw a circle around the numbers they counted to show a pattern.

Name _____

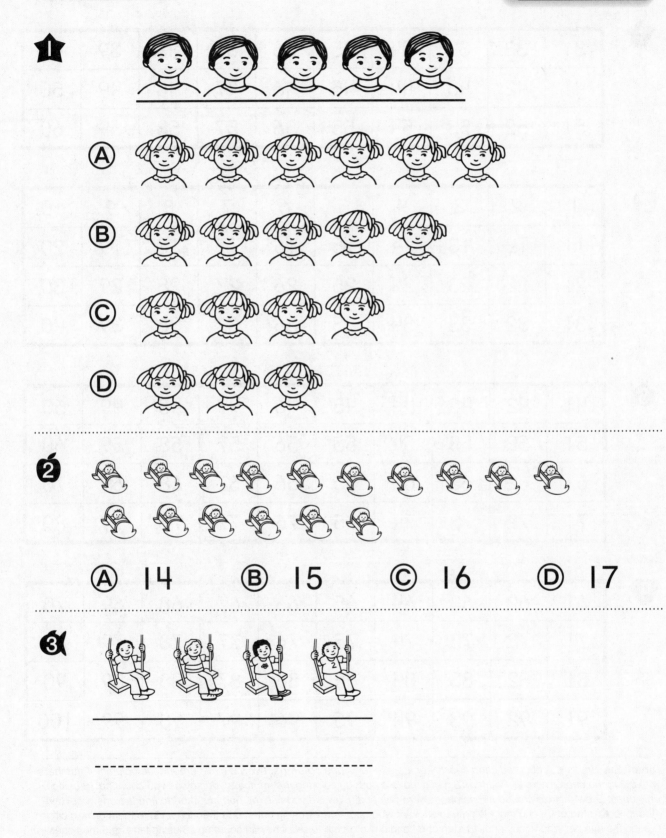

★1

(A)

(B)

(C)

(D)

②

(A) 14   (B) 15   (C) 16   (D) 17

★3

_____

- -

_____

Directions Have students: ★1 mark the picture that shows the same number of girls as boys; ② mark the number that tells how many babies; ★3 count the number of children swinging, and then practice writing the number.

⭐

31	32	33	34	35	36	37	38	39	40
41	42	43	44	45	46	47	48	49	50
51	52	53	54	55	56	57	58	59	60

❷

1	2	3	4	5	6	7	8	9	10
11	12	13	14	15	16	17	18	19	20
21	22	23	(24)	25	26	27	28	29	30
31	32	33	34	35	36	37	38	39	40

❸

41	42	43	44	45	46	47	48	49	50
51	52	53	54	55	56	57	58	59	60
61	62	63	64	65	66	67	68	69	70
71	72	73	74	75	76	77	78	79	80

❹

61	62	63	64	65	66	67	68	69	70
71	72	73	74	75	76	77	78	79	80
81	82	83	84	85	86	87	88	89	90
91	92	93	94	95	96	97	98	99	100

Directions Say: ⭐ *A hundred chart shows numbers in rows and* **columns**. *Draw a circle around the column of numbers with a 3 in the ones place;* ❷ *Point to 12. Let's make a path by coloring the numbers you say as you count up 12 using only ones. Draw a circle around the number where you end. How did you use the number chart to find the answer?* Have students: ❸ start at 44 and make a path to show how to count up 21 using ones, and then tens. Have them draw a circle around the number where they end; ❹ start at 67 and make a path to show how to count up 23 using tens, and then ones. Have them draw a circle around the number where they end, and then explain how they used the number chart to find the answer. **On the Back!** Have students write the numbers 15, 25, 35, and 45, and then write the next 4 numbers to complete the pattern. Students can use a hundred chart to help them.

Helping Hands

Share your thinking while you work.

Start 👥 Put ⬚1 ⬚2 ⬚3 ⬚4 ⬚5 and ⬚6 in a 🛍️.

Get 1 blue square.

Count up ⬚ ⬚.

1	2	3	4	5	6	7	8	9	10
11	12	13	14	15	16	17	18	19	20
21	22	23	24	25	26	27	28	29	30
31	32	33	34	35	36	37	38	39	40
41	42	43	44	45	46	47	48	49	50
51	52	53	54	55	56	57	58	59	60
61	62	63	64	65	66	67	68	69	70
71	72	73	74	75	76	77	78	79	80
81	82	83	84	85	86	87	88	89	90
91	92	93	94	95	96	97	98	99	100

Materials   Number tiles 1, 2, 3, 4, 5, and 6, a bag for the tiles, 1 blue square

Oral Directions   **TRY** Pick 2 tiles. Put the tiles in the spaces at the top of the page. Point to the number 33. Say, "Count up [12] using only ones." Have a partner count up [12], and then put a blue square on the number where they end. Count up [12] together and then tell why the answer is correct.

Put the tiles back in the bag. Switch roles and repeat the activity again. Start at the number 27 this time.

TRY AGAIN If you have time, play again! Choose from these numbers to start counting: 15, 24, 28, 30.

Helping Hands

Partner Talk

Share your thinking while you work.

Start 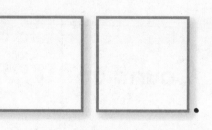 Put 1 2 3 and 4 in a .

Get 1 blue square.

Count up ☐ ☐ .

1	2	3	4	5	6	7	8	9	10
11	12	13	14	15	16	17	18	19	20
21	22	23	24	25	26	27	28	29	30
31	32	33	34	35	36	37	38	39	40
41	42	43	44	45	46	47	48	49	50
51	52	53	54	55	56	57	58	59	60
61	62	63	64	65	66	67	68	69	70
71	72	73	74	75	76	77	78	79	80
81	82	83	84	85	86	87	88	89	90
91	92	93	94	95	96	97	98	99	100

Materials Number tiles 1, 2, 3, and 4, bag for the tiles, 1 blue square

Oral Directions **TRY** Pick 2 tiles. Put the tiles in the spaces at the top of the page. Point to 45. To a partner, say, "Start at 45. Count up 32 by ones and then by tens. What is the end number?" Have a partner begin at the start number, count up 32 aloud, and then explain the strategy he or she used to get to the end number. Cover the end number with the blue square.

Put the tiles back in the bag. Switch roles and repeat the activity again. This time, start at 36.

TRY AGAIN If you have time, play again! This time, start at 20 or 30 and count by ones and then by tens.

Center Game ★★ 11·7

This book belongs to:

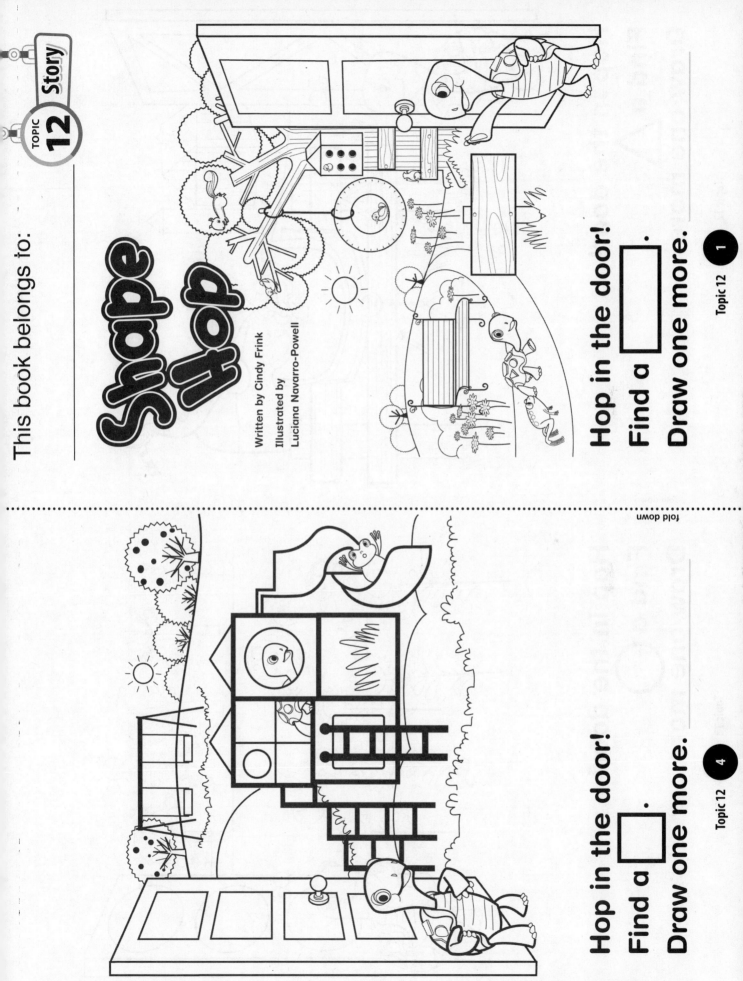

Shape Hop

Written by Cindy Frink

Illustrated by
Luciana Navarro-Powell

Hop in the door!
Find a ☐.
Draw one more.

Topic 12   **1**

fold down

Hop in the door!
Find a ☐.
Draw one more.

Topic 12   **4**

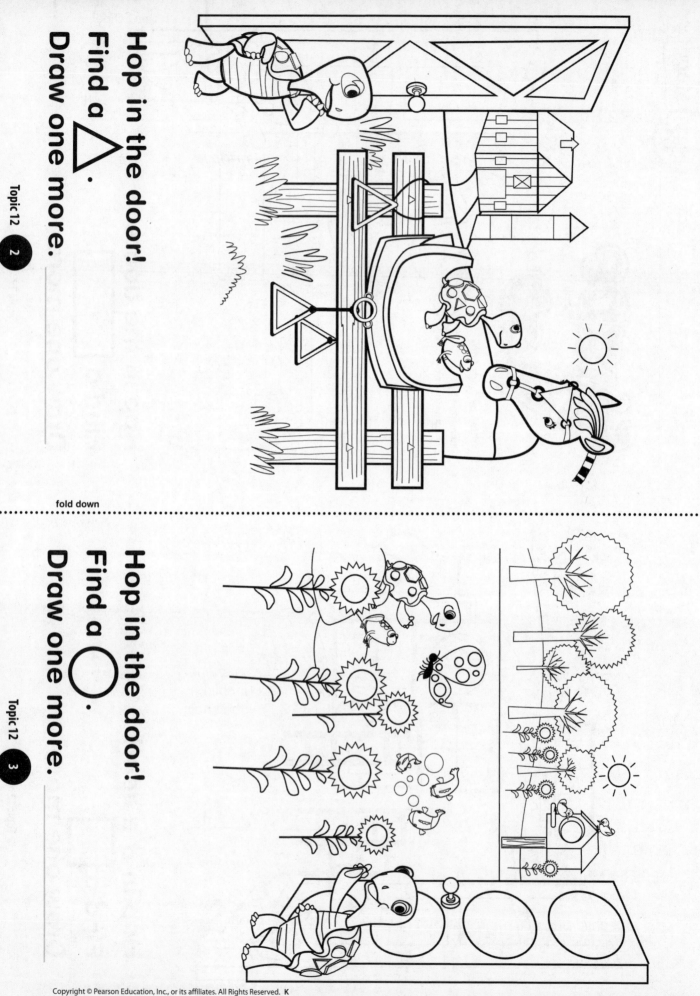

Hop in the door!
Find a △.
Draw one more.

fold down

Hop in the door!
Find a ◯.
Draw one more.

Name _____

Identify and Describe Shapes

Topic 12 Standards
K.G.A.1, K.G.A.2, K.G.A.3, K.G.B.4
See the front of the Student's Edition for complete standards.

Dear Family,

Your child is learning about geometry. In this topic, he or she will learn how to identify and describe shapes. Your child will learn to recognize 2- and 3-dimensional shapes, like circles, rectangles, and cylinders. He or she will also utilize new vocabulary to describe the position and location of shapes.

Location

Here is an activity to do with your child to practice describing locations.

Describe the Position of Shapes

Locate shapes all around your house. Have your child identify the shape, and then describe its location in relationship to other objects in the room. Have your child use the terms *in front of, next to, behind, beside, above,* and *below* to describe where the shape is in relation to the object you choose.

Observe Your Child

Focus on Mathematical Practice 6
Attend to precision.

Help your child become proficient with Mathematical Practice 6. During the activity, encourage your child to use the correct terminology when describing location.

Identificar y describir figuras

Estándares del Tema 12

K.G.A.1, K.G.A.2, K.G.A.3, K.G.B.4
Los estándares completos se encuentran en las páginas preliminares del
Libro del estudiante.

Estimada familia:

Su niño(a) está aprendiendo sobre geometría. En este tema, aprenderá a identificar
y describir figuras. Su niño(a) aprenderá a reconocer figuras bidimensionales y
tridimensionales, como círculos, rectángulos y cilindros. También aprenderá a usar
vocabulario nuevo para describir la posición y ubicación de las figuras.

Ubicación

Arriba

Junto a

Debajo

Aquí se presenta una actividad para hacer con su niño(a) y practicar la descripción
de ubicaciones.

Describir la posición de las figuras

Ubiquen las figuras en su casa. Pídale a su niño(a) que identifique la figura y luego,
describa su ubicación en relación con otros objetos de la habitación. Pídale a su niño(a) que
use los términos *frente a, junto a, atrás de, al lado de, arriba de* y *debajo de* para describir
en dónde está la figura en relación al objeto que escoja.

Observe a su niño(a)

Enfoque en la Práctica matemática 6:
Prestar atención a la precisión.

Ayude a su niño(a) a adquirir competencia en la Práctica matemática 6. Durante la
actividad, anime a su niño(a) a usar el vocabulario correcto al describir la ubicación.

Name _____

Shapes in the World

Directions Say: *Did you know that everyday objects can be described by their shape? For example, some books are shaped like squares, and some are shaped like rectangles. What other everyday objects can you describe by their shape?* ★–❹ Have students draw a circle around the shape that matches the shape of the object on the left. **Extension** Have students find objects in the classroom that are shaped like a circle and a square, and then draw them.

Name _____

Objects in the Environment

Directions Say: *Did you know that most everyday objects are solid figures? Some trashcans and vases are cylinders. Soccer and golf balls are spheres. What other everyday objects can you think of?* Have students: ❶ and ❷ look at the solid figure on the left, and then draw a circle around the object on the right that is the same solid figure; ❸ draw a circle around the 4 objects that are the same solid figure, and then name the solid figure. **Extension:** Have students draw two objects that are NOT cylinders.

Math and Science Activity **12·6**

Name _____

1

Ⓐ $4 + 3 = 7$

Ⓑ $3 + 3 = 6$

Ⓒ $3 + 2 = 5$

Ⓓ $1 + 2 = 3$

2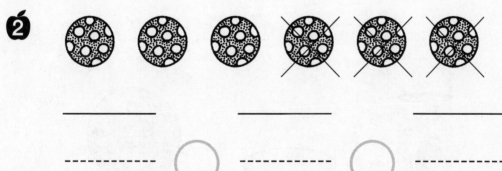

_____   _____   _____

- - - - - - ◯ - - - - - - ◯ - - - - - -

_____   _____   _____

Directions Have students: **1** mark the equation that tells about joining the 2 groups of milk; **2** write an equation that tells how many marbles are left.

Name _____

Directions Say: ⭐ *Flat shapes can also be called* **two-dimensional shapes.** *Look at the flat shapes. Draw an object in the classroom that looks like each flat shape.* Have students describe the shapes and objects; ② *Look at the objects. The piece of notebook paper is flat. Which other object is flat? Draw a circle around the flat objects. The tissue box is solid. Mark an X on the objects that are solid.* ③ *and* ④ Have students draw a circle around the objects that are flat, and mark an X on the objects that are solid. **On the Back!** Have students draw a picture of an object that is flat and an object that is solid. Have them describe the objects.

1 $1 + 7 = ?$

Ⓐ 7

Ⓑ 8

Ⓒ 9

Ⓓ 11

2

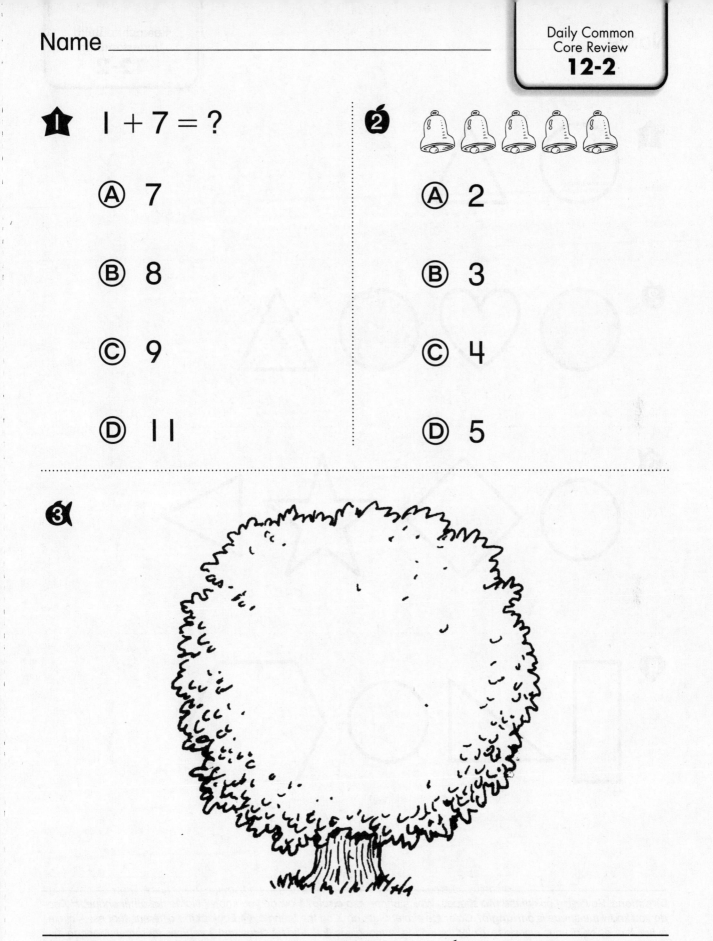

Ⓐ 2

Ⓑ 3

Ⓒ 4

Ⓓ 5

3

Directions Have students: **1** mark the number that completes the equation; **2** mark the number that tells how many bells; **3** draw 6 birds in the tree.

Name _____

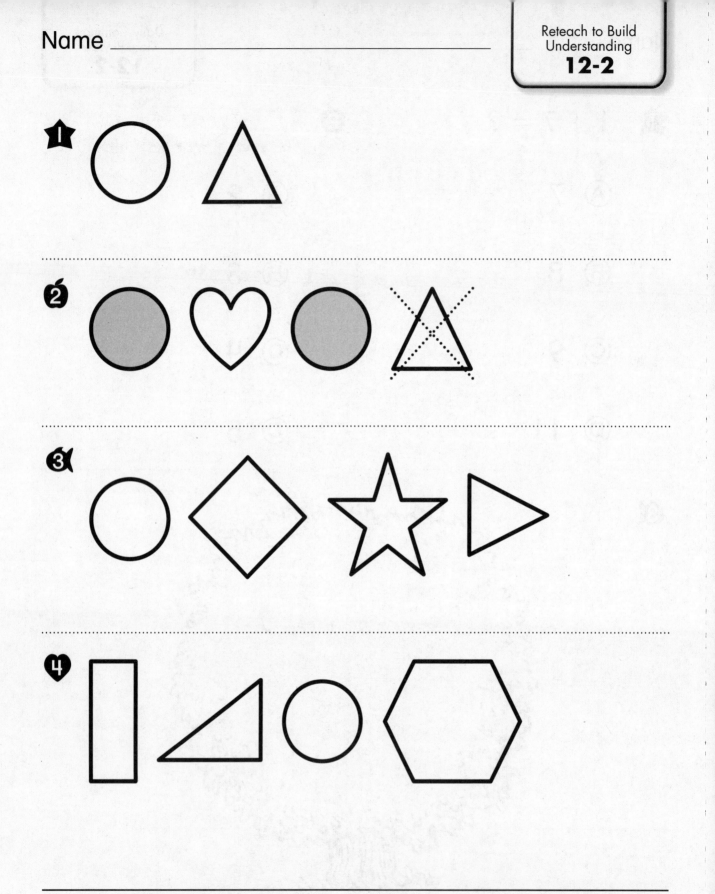

Directions Say: ❶ *Look at the two shapes. Which shape is a **circle**? How do you know? Name the other shape. How do you know the shape is a **triangle**? Color the circle. Mark an X on the triangle;* ❷ *Look at the different shapes. A circle is flat. It does NOT have any sides. Color the circles. A triangle is flat. It has 3 sides and 3 vertices (corners). Mark an X on the triangle.* ❸ *and* ❹ *Have students color the circles and mark an X on the triangles.* **On the Back!** *Have students draw 3 circles of different sizes and 3 triangles of different sizes.*

Cover Three

Start 👫 Put ⓪ and ③ in a 🛍.

Get 6 red squares.
Get 6 blue squares.

Pick	Cover
⓪	○
③	△

To win, get: ■■■ or ■ or ■ or ■
■ ■ ■
■ ■ ■

Materials Number tiles 0 and 3, paper bag, 6 red squares, 6 blue squares

Oral Directions **TRY** Give 6 red squares to one player. Give 6 blue squares to the other player. Take turns. Pick a tile from the bag. Say the number. Name the shape next to that number. Look on the game board. Find a shape that has the same name. Trace that shape with your finger. If the shape is a circle, tell why it is a circle. If the shape is a triangle, tell why it is a triangle. Cover that shape with a square. Put the tile back in the bag. Take turns until one player wins. You can see the ways to win below the game board.

TRY AGAIN If you have time, play again!

Cover Three

Start 👥 Put ⓪ and ③ in a 🛍.

Get 6 red squares.
Get 6 blue squares.

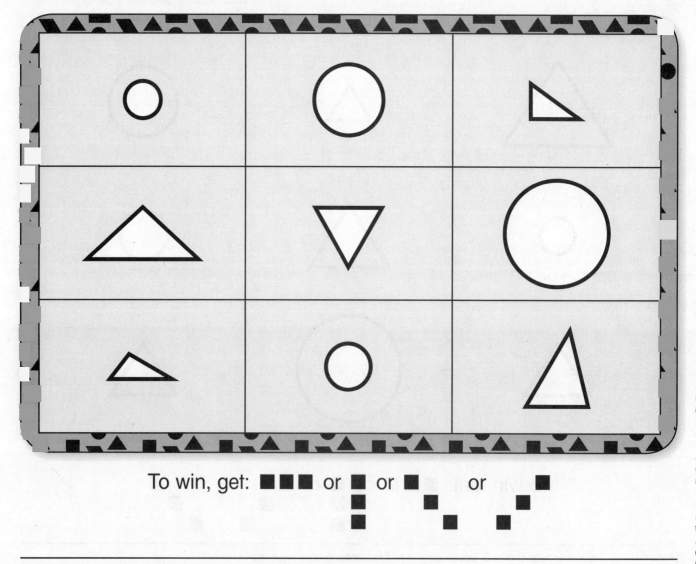

To win, get: ■■■ or ■ or ■ or ■

Materials Number tiles 0 and 3, paper bag, 6 red squares, 6 blue squares

Oral Directions **TRY** Give 6 red squares to one player. Give 6 blue squares to the other player. Take turns. Pick a tile from the bag. Say the number. Look on the game board. Find a shape with that number of vertices. Trace that shape. Name that shape. Then use a square to cover that shape. Put the tile back in the bag. Take turns until one player wins. You can see the ways to win below the game board.

TRY AGAIN If you have time, play again!

Name _____

⭐1️⃣ $10 - \underline{\ ?\ } = 4$

$10 - 4 = \underline{\ ?\ }$

Ⓐ 3

Ⓑ 5

Ⓒ 6

Ⓓ 8

🍎2️⃣

Ⓐ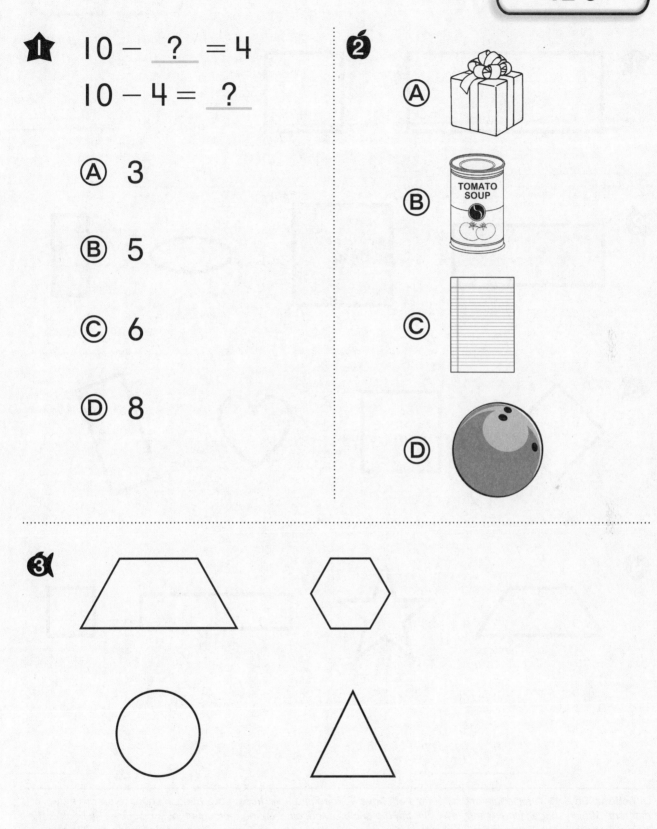

Ⓑ

Ⓒ

Ⓓ

3️⃣

Directions Have students: ⭐1️⃣ mark the number that completes the equations; 🍎2️⃣ mark the picture that is NOT a solid;
3️⃣ draw a circle around the triangle.

Name _____

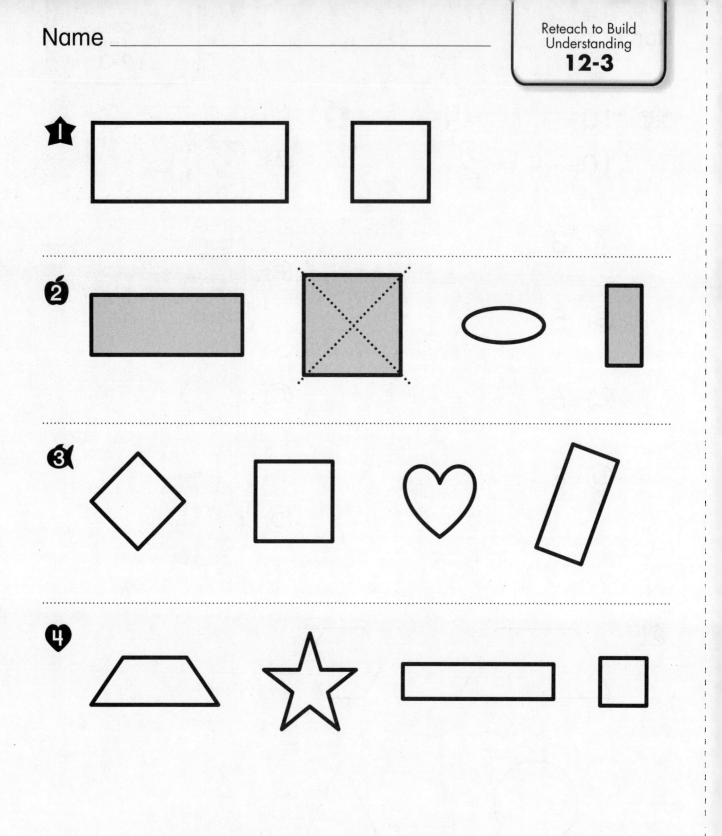

Directions Say: ⭐ *A rectangle and a square both have 4 **sides** and 4 **vertices**. Look at each shape. How are they different? Which shape is the rectangle? Color the rectangles. Mark an X on the rectangle that is a square;* 🍎 *Look at the different shapes. A rectangle is flat. How many sides does a rectangle have? A square is a special rectangle. It is also flat. How is a square different from a rectangle? How many rectangles are there? Color them. How many of the rectangles are squares? Mark an X on the rectangle that is a square.* ⭐ *and* ❤ *Have students color the rectangles and mark an X on the rectangles that are squares.* **On the Back!** *Have students draw 3 squares of different sizes and 3 rectangles of different sizes.*

Look and See

Start 👫 Put ⬜1 ⬜2 ⬜3 ⬜4 ⬜5 in a 🛍.

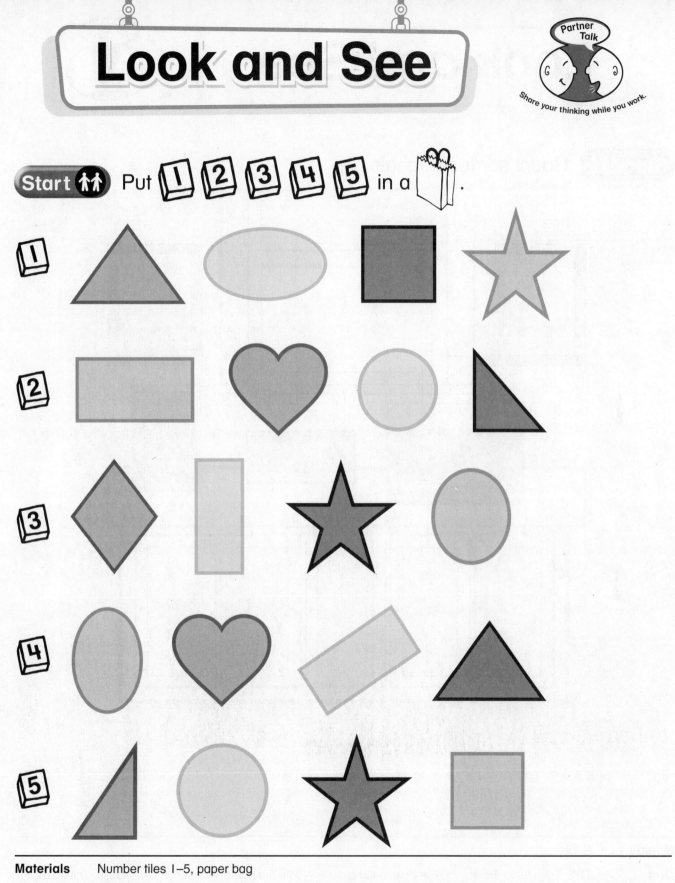

Materials   Number tiles 1–5, paper bag

Oral Directions   **TRY** Take turns. Pick a tile from the bag. Find the row of shapes next to your number. Use your finger to trace the rectangle in that row. Tell your partner if that rectangle is a square or if it is NOT a square. Do NOT put the tile back in the bag. Take turns until the bag of tiles is empty.

TRY AGAIN If you have time, put the tiles back in the bag. Begin again!

Look and See

Start 👥 Count some rectangles.

Materials	None
Oral Directions	**TRY** Take turns. Point to a rectangle in the picture. Name the object that has that rectangle. Tell your partner if that rectangle is or is NOT a square.
	TRY AGAIN If you have time, take turns. On your turn, tell your partner about something else that you can show by drawing a rectangle that is NOT a square. Or, tell your partner about something else that you can show by drawing a rectangle that is a square.

Name _____

1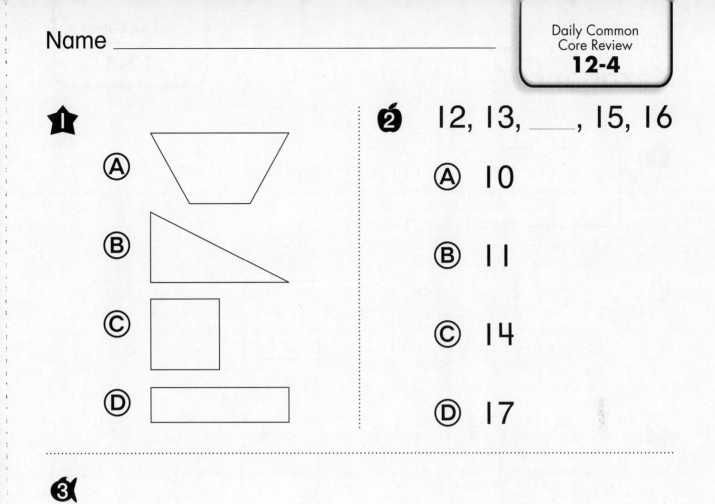

Ⓐ

Ⓑ

Ⓒ

Ⓓ

2 12, 13, ____, 15, 16

Ⓐ 10

Ⓑ 11

Ⓒ 14

Ⓓ 17

3

Directions Have students: **1** mark the square; **2** mark the missing number; **3** draw 2 different rectangles.

 D 12•4

Name _____

Hexagons

1 [rectangle and hexagon shapes]

2 [star, shaded hexagon, square, inverted triangle]

3 [hexagon, trapezoid, hexagon, oval]

4 [right triangle, hexagon, rectangle, diamond]

5 [beach ball, traffic cone, shaded hexagon, bucket]

Directions Say: **1** *A* **hexagon** *has 6 sides. Color the hexagon. Name the other shape. How are the shapes different?*
2 *Look at the shapes. Which shape is a hexagon? How do you know? Color the hexagon.* Have students: **3** and **4**
color the hexagon(s) in each row; **5** draw a circle around the object that looks like a hexagon. **On the Back!** Have
students draw a hexagon, a circle, and a square.

Name _____

1

Ⓐ

Ⓑ

Ⓒ

Ⓓ

2

Ⓐ

Ⓑ

Ⓒ

Ⓓ

3

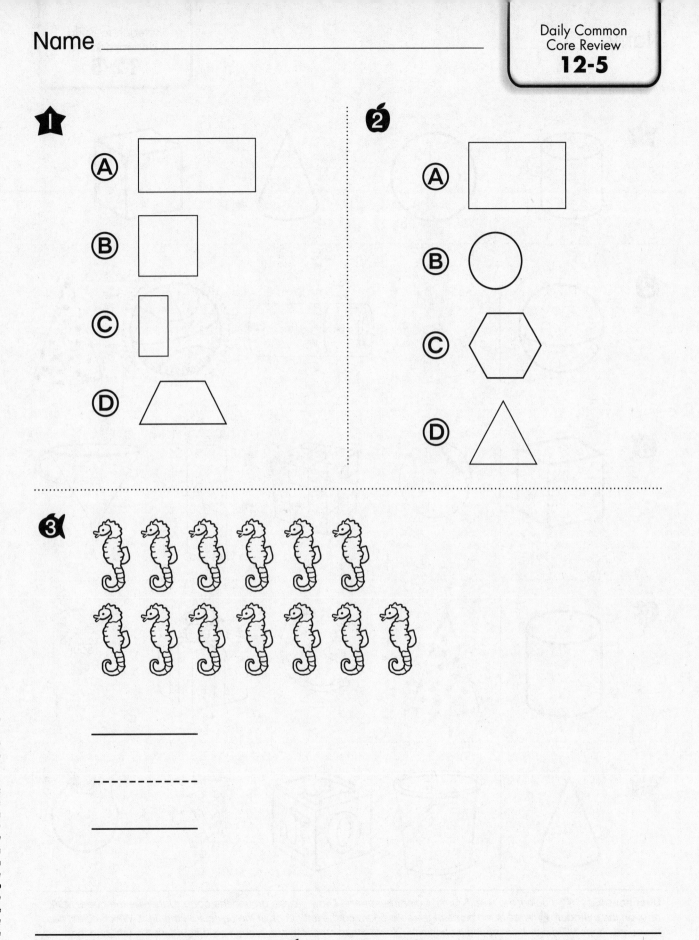

_____

- - - - - - - - - -

_____

Directions Have students: **1** mark the square; **2** mark the rectangle; **3** count the seahorses, and then write the number that tells how many.

Name _____

Directions Say: ⭐ *Look at the solid figures. Color the **sphere**. Draw a circle around the **cone**. Underline the **cube**. Mark an X on the **cylinder**;* ② *What is the name of the solid figure on the left? Look at the objects on the right. Which object has the same shape? Draw a circle around that object.* ❸–✋ *Have students name each solid figure on the left, and then draw a circle around the object that has the same shape.* **On the Back!** *Have students draw a picture of an object that has the shape of a cube, a sphere, a cone, or a cylinder, and then name the solid figure.*

 R 12·5

Play a Game

Start 👥 Get .

Get 1 blue square.
Get 1 red square.

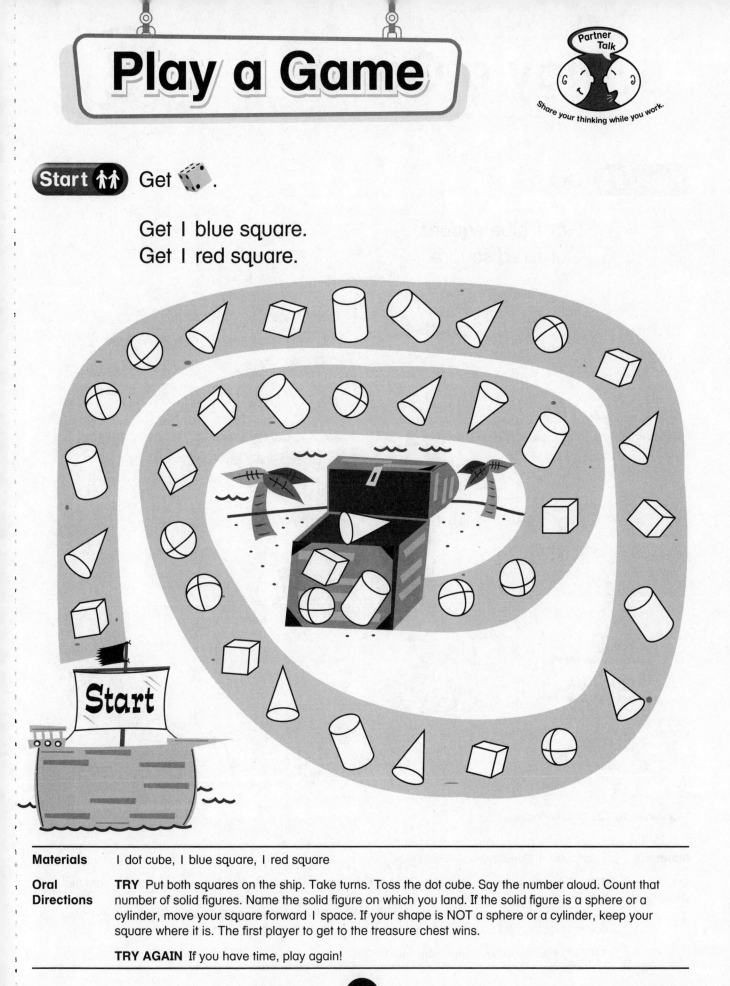

Materials	1 dot cube, 1 blue square, 1 red square
Oral Directions	**TRY** Put both squares on the ship. Take turns. Toss the dot cube. Say the number aloud. Count that number of solid figures. Name the solid figure on which you land. If the solid figure is a sphere or a cylinder, move your square forward 1 space. If your shape is NOT a sphere or a cylinder, keep your square where it is. The first player to get to the treasure chest wins.
	TRY AGAIN If you have time, play again!

Play a Game

Start 👥 Get 🎲.

Get 1 blue square.
Get 1 red square.

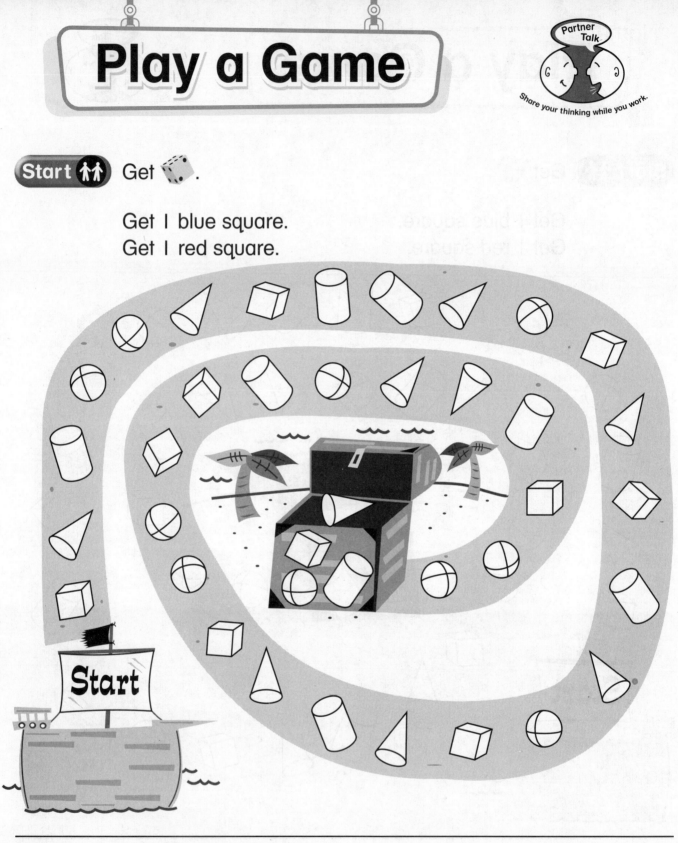

Materials	1 dot cube, 1 blue square, 1 red square
Oral Directions	**TRY** Put both squares on the ship. Take turns. Toss the dot cube. Say the number aloud. Count that number of solid figures. Name the solid figure on which you land. Name any object you have seen outside, in your classroom, or at home that looks like that solid figure. Then cover the figure with your colored square. The first player to get to the treasure chest wins.
	TRY AGAIN If you have time, play again!

Name _____

1

Ⓐ △

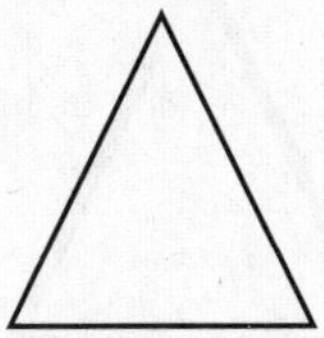

Ⓒ ▢

Ⓑ ◯

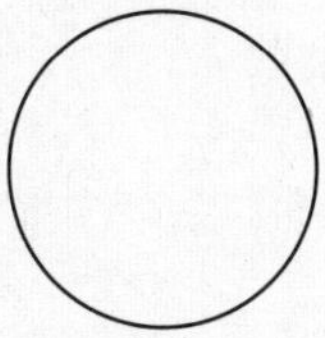

Ⓓ ☆

· ·

2

· ·

3

8 = _____ $+$ _____

Directions Have students: **1** mark the circle; **2** draw an object shaped like a square; **3** draw a circle around 2 groups of yo-yos to show a number pair for 8, and then complete the equation to show a way to break apart 8.

Name _____

Directions Say: ⭐ *Look at the flat and solid shapes. Color the* **sphere**. *Draw a circle around the* **square**. *Underline the* **triangle**. *Mark an X on the* **cylinder**; 🍎 *Look at the picture. Which objects in the picture are flat? Draw a circle around the objects that are flat. Which objects are solid? Mark an X on the objects that are solid.* ⭐ *Have students point to objects in the picture and name their shape. Then have them draw a circle around the objects that look like a cylinder and mark an X on the objects that look like a cube.* **On the Back!** *Have students draw a picture of a park. Have them include objects that are shaped like a sphere and objects that are shaped like a rectangle.*

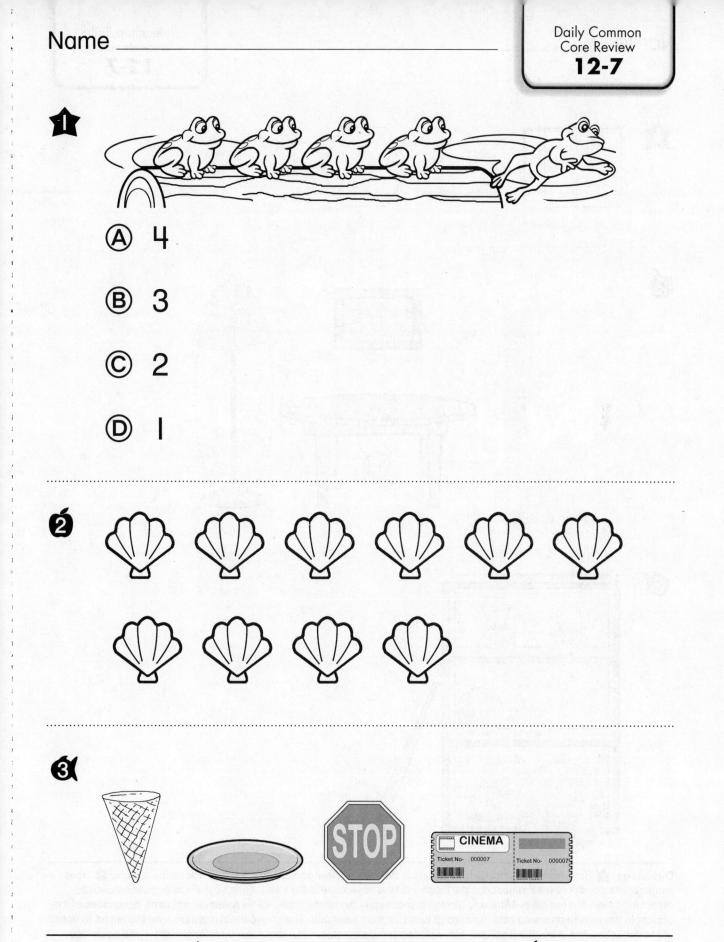

1

(A) 4

(B) 3

(C) 2

(D) 1

2

3

STOP

CINEMA
Ticket No- 000007
Ticket No- 000007

Directions Have students: **1** mark the number that tells how many frogs are left on the log; **2** draw a circle around the row of shells that is less in number than the other row of shells; **3** draw a circle around the object that is NOT flat.

Name _____

⭐

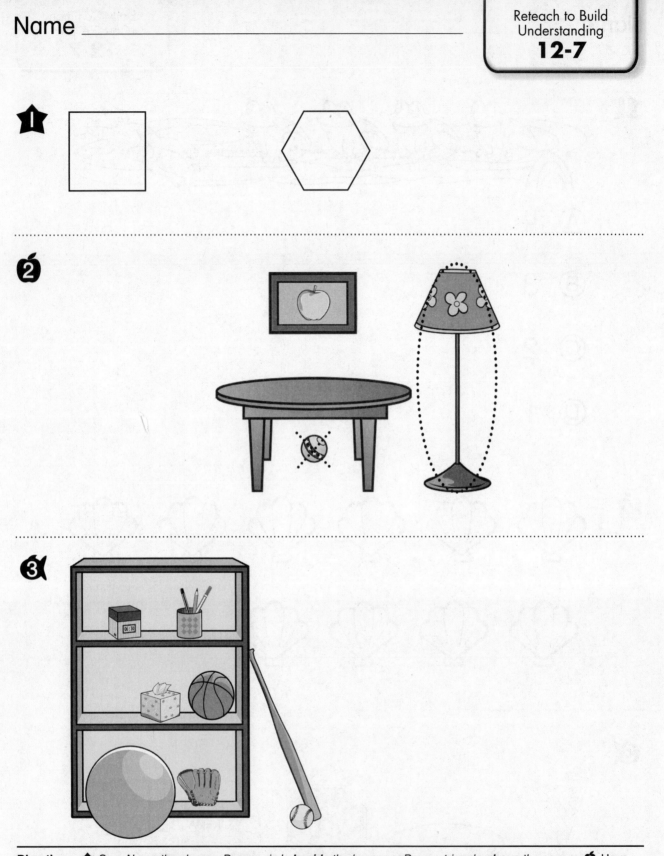

Directions ⭐ Say: *Name the shapes. Draw a circle **beside** the hexagon. Draw a triangle **above** the square.* ❷ Have students use position words to describe the location of the objects near the table. Then say: *Draw a circle around the object that is next to the table. Mark an X on the object that is below the table.* ❸ Have students name the shapes of the objects in the picture and use position words to describe their locations. Then have them mark an X on the object in front of the bookcase that looks like a sphere. Have students draw an object that looks like a rectangle above the bookcase. **On the Back!** Have students draw a picture of a desk. Have them draw an object that looks like a circle above the desk and an object that looks like a cylinder next to the desk.

Play a Game

Start 👫 Put ⬜1 ⬜2 in a 🛍️ .

Get 5 red squares.
Get 5 blue squares.

Put your tile here.

Materials 5 red squares, 5 blue squares, number tiles 1–2, paper bag

Oral Directions **TRY** Look at the picture. Name some objects that are in front of the fence. Name some objects that are behind the fence. Give 5 red squares to one player. Give 5 blue squares to the other player. Pick a tile. If you pick a 1, the player with blue squares says the word "in front of," names something that is in front of the fence, and then puts a square on it. If you pick a 2, the player with red squares says the word "behind," names something that is behind the fence, and then puts a square on it. Put the tile back in the bag. Keep playing until one player uses all 5 squares and wins the game.

TRY AGAIN If you have time, play again!

Play a Game

Start 👫 Put ① ② in a 🛍 .

Get 7 red squares.
Get 7 blue squares.

Put your tile here.

Materials 7 red squares, 7 blue squares, number tiles 1–2, paper bag

Oral Directions **TRY** Look at the picture. Name some objects that are in front of the fence. Name some objects that are behind the fence. Give 7 red squares to one player. Give 7 blue squares to the other player. Pick a tile. Take turns. If you pick a 1, point to 1 picture. Say "in front of" or "behind" to tell your partner where it is. For example, you could say, "The dog is in front of the fence." Then put a square on your picture. If you pick a 2, point to 2 pictures. Say "in front of" or "behind" to tell your partner where they are. Then place a square on each picture. Put the tile back in the bag. Play until one player uses all 7 squares and wins the game.

TRY AGAIN If you have time, talk about some things that are in front of the teacher's desk and some things that are behind the teacher's desk. Or, play the game again!

Center Game ★★ 12·7

Name _____

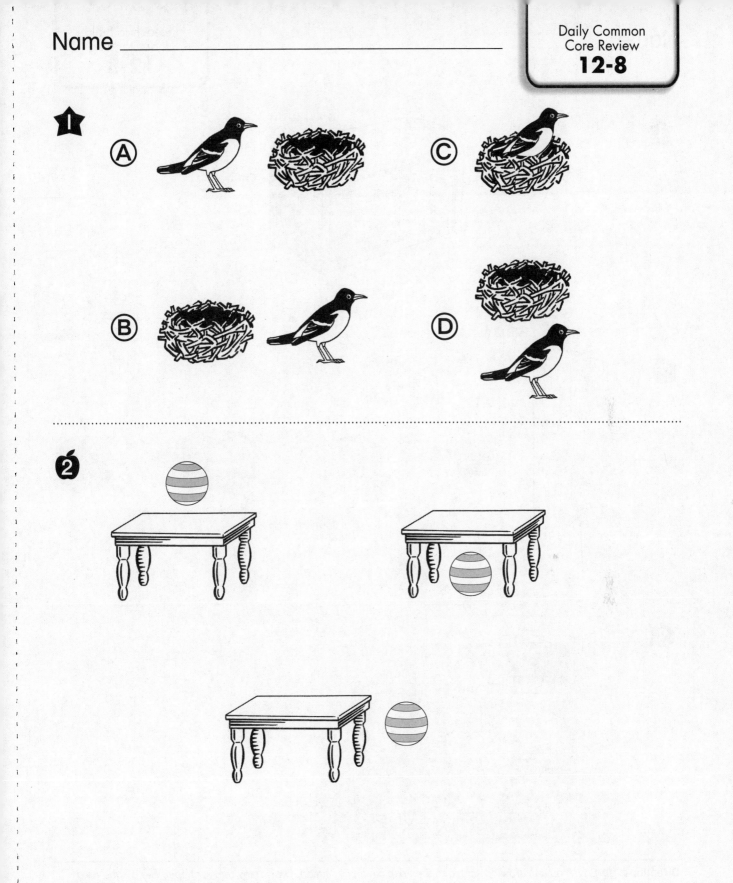

1

Ⓐ

Ⓒ

Ⓑ

Ⓓ

2

Directions Have students: **1** mark the bird below the nest; **2** draw a circle around the picture that shows the ball next to the table.

D 12·8

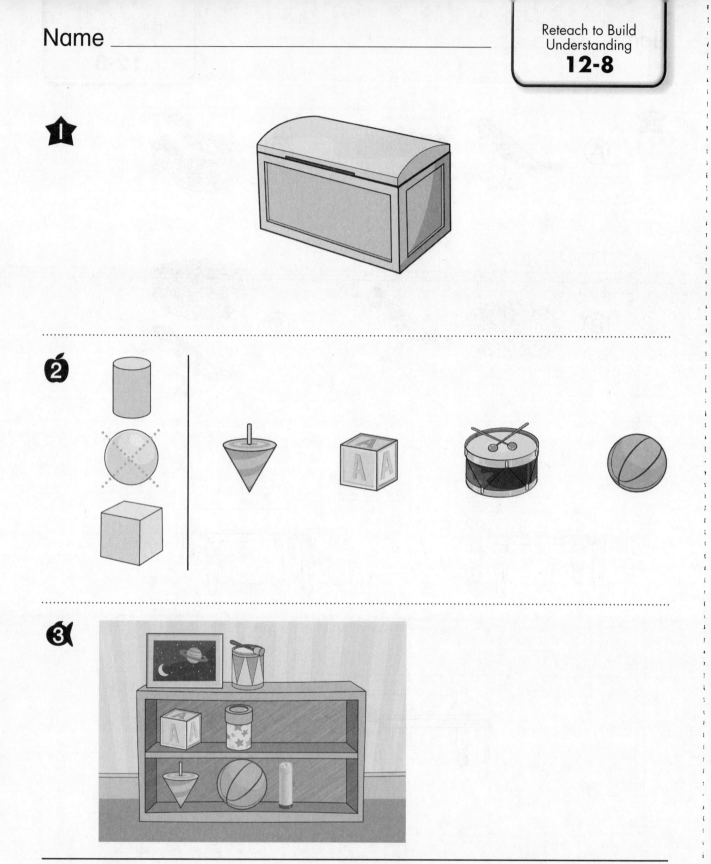

Directions ⭐ Say: *You can draw objects, and then explain their location. Draw a toy that is shaped like a cube **next to** the toy chest. Draw a toy that is shaped like a sphere **above** the toy chest.* Have students: ❷ name the solid figures on the left. Then say: *Which object is NOT beside the block? Which solid figure is shaped like that object? Mark an X on the sphere.* Have students explain why a cylinder or cube is NOT the right answer; ❸ name the shape of the objects in the picture. Then have them mark an X on the object that is below the drum, and is next to the object that is shaped like a cube. Have students explain how they decided which shape to mark. **On the Back!** Have students draw a picture that shows an object that is shaped like a sphere below a desk and a picture above the desk.

This book belongs to:

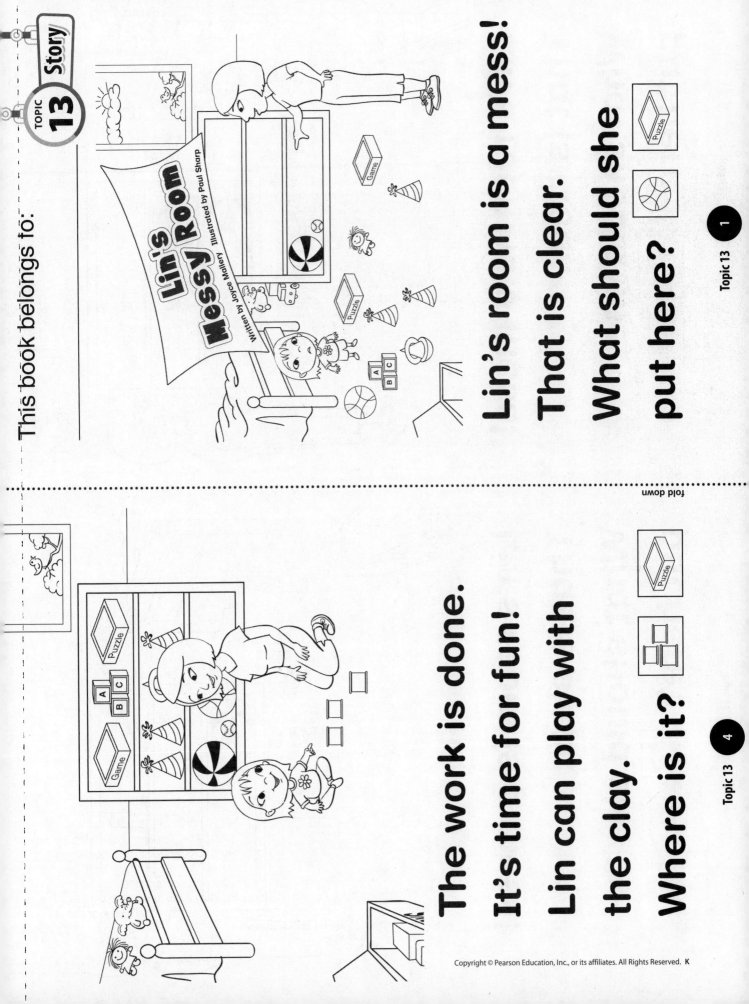

Lin's Messy Room

Written by Joyce Mallery   Illustrated by Paul Sharp

Lin's room is a mess!
That is clear.
What should she
put here?

Topic 13   1

fold down

The work is done.
It's time for fun!
Lin can play with
the clay.
Where is it?

Topic 13   4

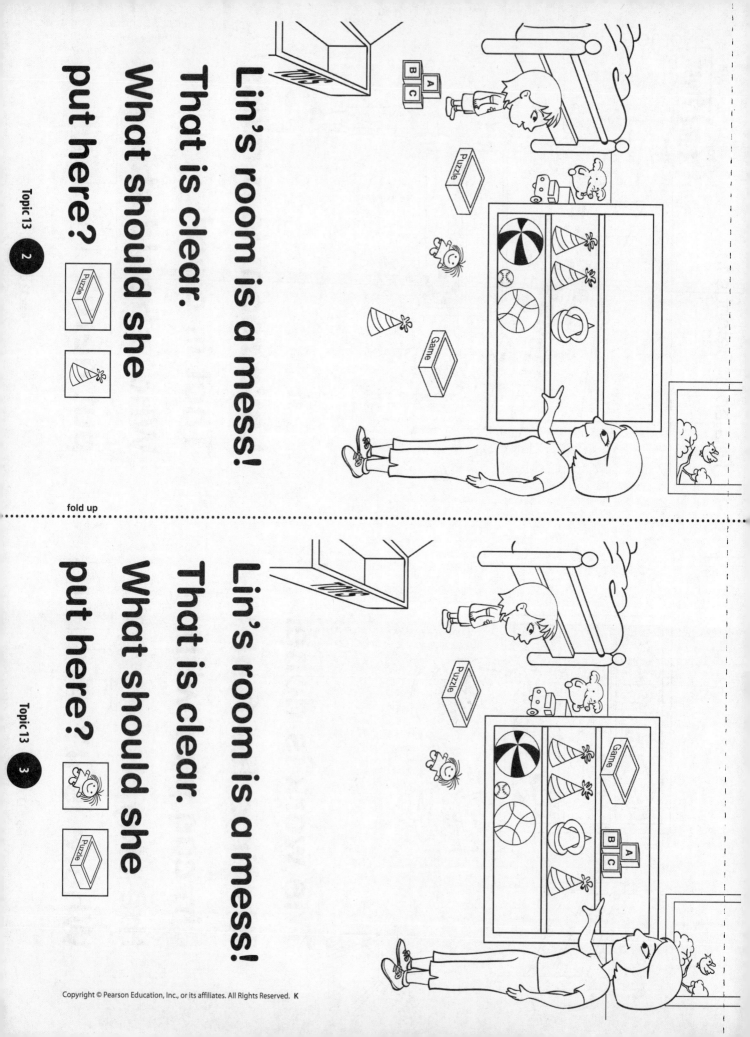

Lin's room is a mess!

That is clear.

What should she put here?

Puzzle

fold up

Lin's room is a mess!

That is clear.

What should she put here?

Puzzle

Name _____

Analyze, Compare, and Create Shapes

Topic 13 Standards
K.G.A.3, K.G.B.4, K.G.B.5, K.G.B.6
See the front of the Student's Edition for complete standards.

Dear Family,

Your child is continuing to learn about geometry. In this topic, he or she will work with both 2-dimensional and 3-dimensional shapes to create other shapes. He or she will also learn to use pattern blocks of different shapes to make new shapes, and how to use solid figures and materials to make new shapes.

Solid Shapes
Use solid figures to create
new shapes, and then tell what
figures were used to make the
new shape.

Here is an activity to do with your child to practice identifying solid shapes.

Make a Shape

Provide craft sticks, pipe cleaners, or string for your child to make shapes with. Name a shape and have your child draw that shape on a piece of paper. Have your child make that same shape using the materials you provided. Repeat using the following shapes: circle, square, rectangle, triangle, hexagon.

Observe Your Child

Focus on Mathematical Practice 1:
Make sense of problems and persevere in solving them.

Help your child become proficient with Mathematical Practice 1. During this activity, ask your child which materials he or she could use to make a circle. Have your child make the circle using the material and ask why he or she chose that material.

Nombre _____

Analizar, comparar y crear figuras

Estándares del Tema 13

K.G.A.3, K.G.B.4, K.G.B.5, K.G.B.6

Los estándares completos se encuentran en las páginas preliminares del
Libro del estudiante.

Estimada familia:

Su niño(a) está aprendiendo sobre geometría. En este tema, él o ella trabajará con figuras bidimensionales y tridimensionales para crear otras figuras. Aprenderá a usar bloques de patrón de diferentes figuras para crear otras figuras. También aprenderá a usar sólidos y materiales para hacer nuevas figuras.

Sólidos
Usen sólidos para crear
figuras nuevas y luego,
digan qué sólidos usaron
para crear las nuevas figuras.

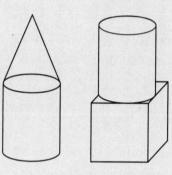

Aquí se presenta una actividad que puede hacer con su niño(a) para practicar la identificación de los sólidos.

Hacer una figura

Dé a su niño(a) palillos de manualidades, limpiapipas o cuerda para hacer figuras con ellos. Nombre una figura y pídale a su niño(a) que dibuje esa figura en un papel y luego, construya la misma figura usando los materiales que le dio. Repita usando las figuras siguientes: círculo, cuadrado, rectángulo, triángulo, hexágono.

Observe a su niño(a)

Enfoque en la Práctica matemática 1:
Entender problemas y perseverar en resolverlos.

Ayude a su niño(a) a adquirir competencia en la Práctica matemática 1. Durante esta actividad, pregúntele a su niño(a) qué materiales podría usar para hacer un círculo. Pídale que construya el círculo usando el material y pregúnte por qué escogió ese material.

Name _____

Shapes

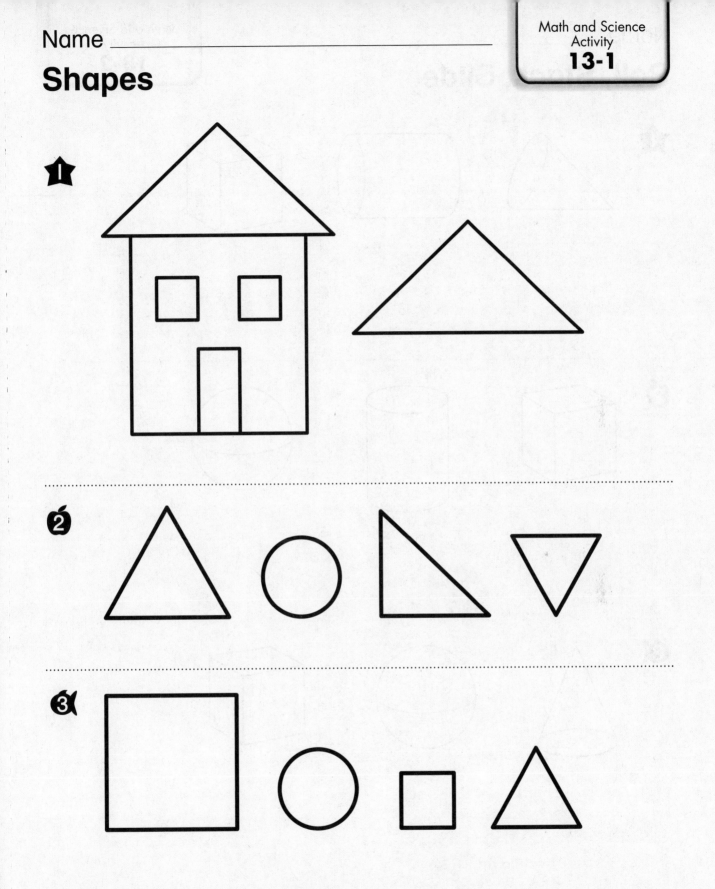

Directions Say: *Did you know that scientists sometimes sort objects by how they are the same and how they are different?*
Have students: ① draw a circle around the part of the house that matches the shape on the right; ② draw a circle around
the shape that does NOT belong with the others; ③ draw a circle around the 2 shapes that have the same shape.
Extension Have students draw 3 objects that are shaped like a circle.

Name _____

Roll, Stack, Slide

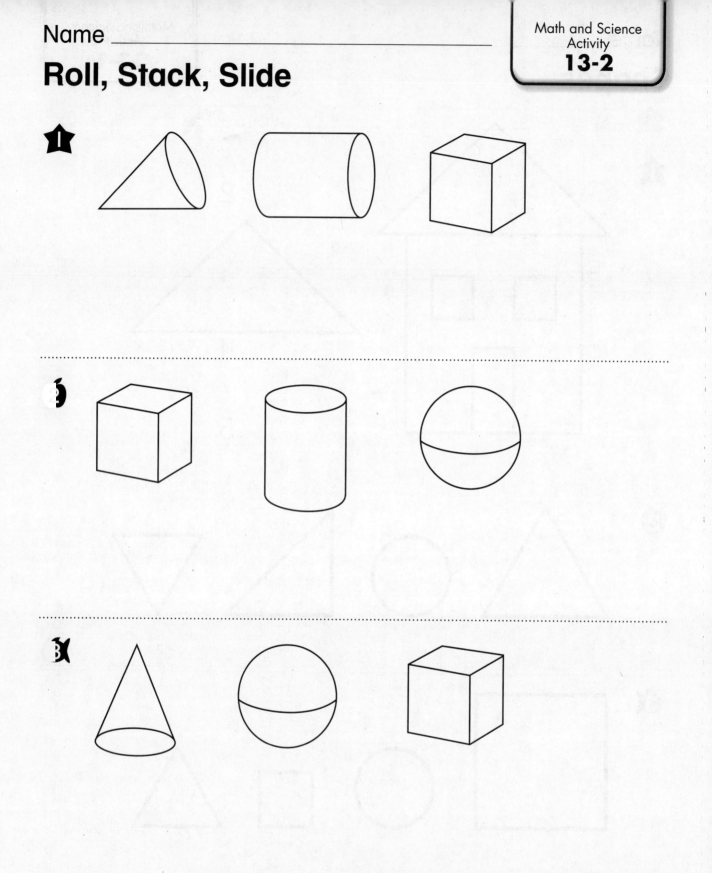

1

2

3

Directions Say: *Did you know that scientists can sort objects by how they move? Solid figures can be sorted by how they move, too. They can roll, stack, or slide.* Have students: **1** mark an X on the solid figure that does NOT roll; **2** draw a circle around the solid figures that can be stacked; **3** mark an X on the solid figure that does NOT slide.
Extension Have students draw 3 objects that can be found in the classroom: I that rolls, I that stacks, and I that slides.

Name _____

 1 $4 + 5 = ?$

    (A) 1

    (B) 4

    (C) 5

    (D) 9

2

    (A) 2

    (B) 3

    (C) 4

    (D) 5

3

Directions Have students: **1** mark the sum of the equation; **2** mark the number that tells how many birds are left; **3** mark an X on the objects that do NOT look like a cylinder.

 D 13·1

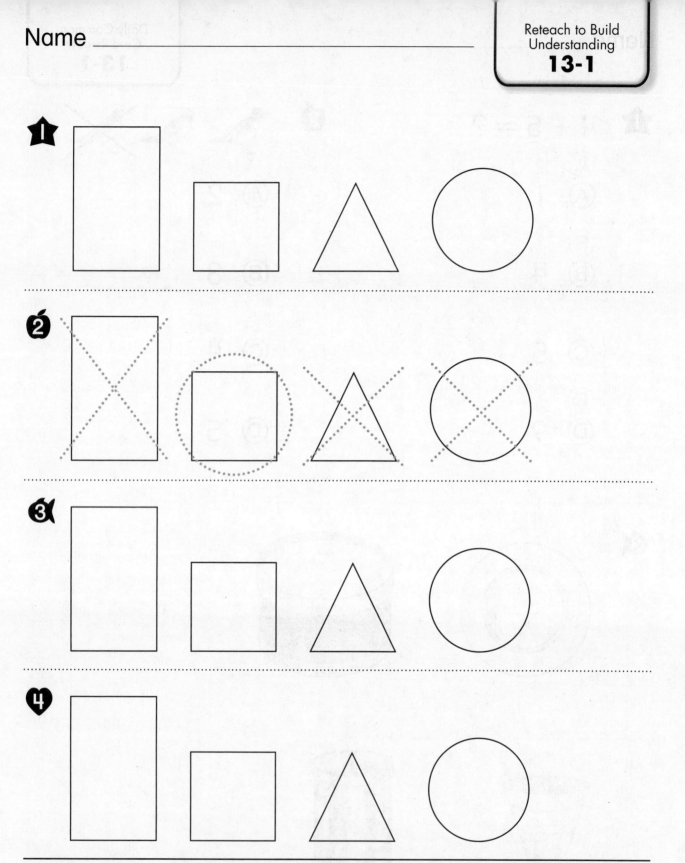

⭐ ①

❷ ②

③

④

Directions Say: ⭐ *Look at the shapes. What shapes do you see? Color the* **circle** *orange, the* **square** *blue, the* **rectangle** *green, and the* **triangle** *red;* ❷ *You can use what you know about shapes to find a mystery shape. Listen to the clues. After each clue, mark an X on any shape that does NOT fit the clue. I have 4 corners. My sides are all the same length. What shape am I? Draw a circle around the mystery shape.* Have students listen to the clues, mark an X on any shape that does NOT fit the clue, and then draw a circle around the shape that fits all of the clues. Say: ③ *I am NOT round. I have 3 sides. What shape am I?* ④ *I do NOT have 4 sides. I have 0 vertices. Which shape am I?* **On the Back!** Have students draw a square, rectangle, circle, or triangle, and then describe the shape using words like *sides* and *vertices*.

Name ____________________

1

Ⓐ 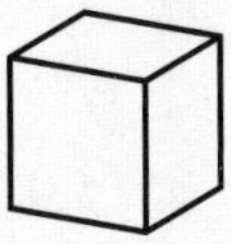

Ⓑ 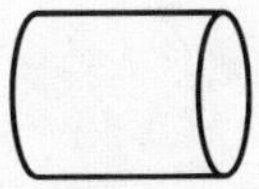

Ⓒ 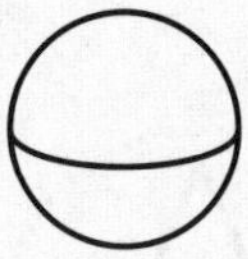

Ⓓ 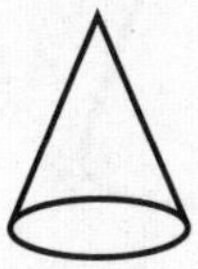

2

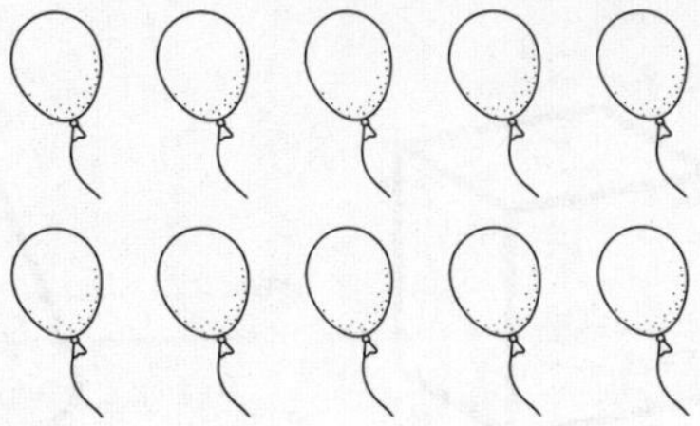

Ⓐ 10

Ⓑ 9

Ⓒ 8

Ⓓ 5

3

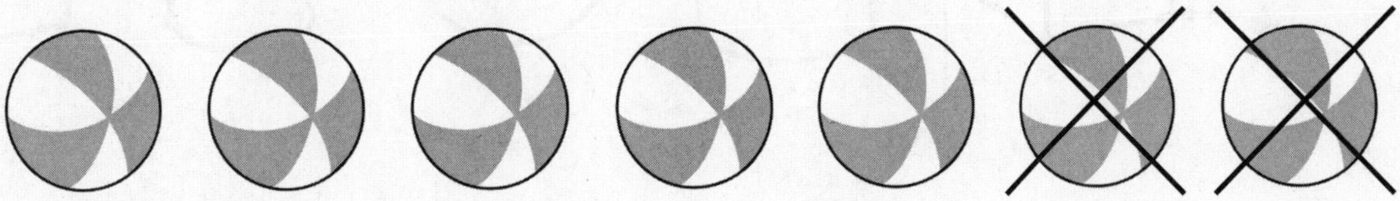

_____ − _____ = _____

Directions Have students: **1** mark the sphere; **2** mark the number that tells how many balloons; **3** write an equation to match the picture.

Name _____

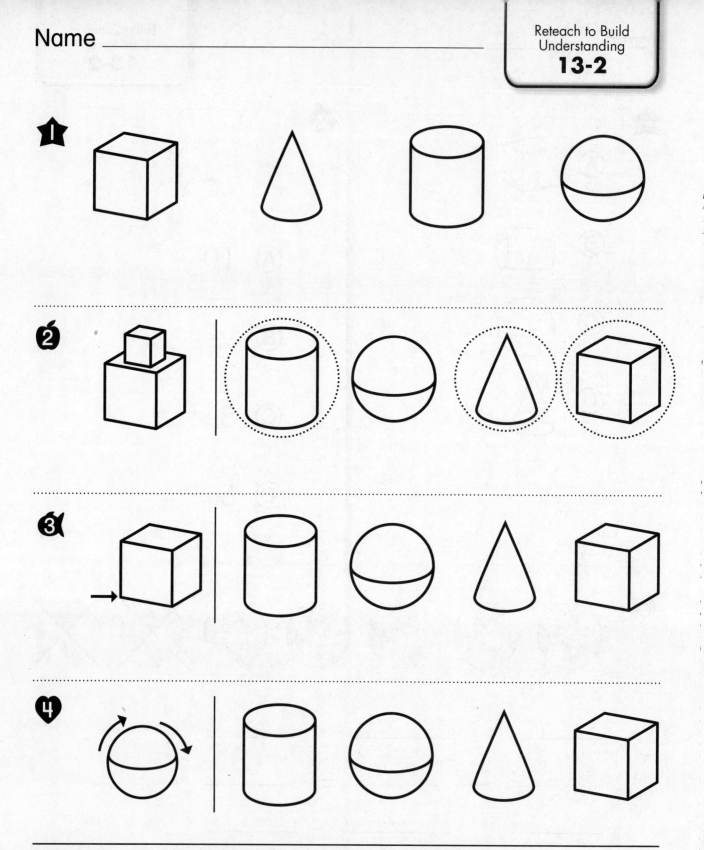

Directions ⭐ Say: *These **three-dimensional shapes** can also be called* solid figures. *Color the sphere blue. Color the cylinder green. Draw a circle around the cube. Draw a line below the cone.* ② *Point to the solid figures on the left. Say: These solid figures are stacked. The small cube is on top of a large cube. Solid figures with flat surfaces can stack. Now look at the other solid figures. Draw a circle around the solid figures that can stack. Say:* ③ *Look at the solid figure on the left. This solid figure can slide. It has a flat surface. Draw a circle around the other solid figures that can slide;* ④ *Look at the solid figure on the left. This solid figure can roll. It does NOT have a flat surface. Draw a circle around the other solid figures that can roll.* **On the Back!** *Draw a picture that shows a solid figure that can roll, a solid figure that can slide, and a solid figure that can stack.*

Name _____

1 ☆ ☆ ☆ ☆ ☆
☆ ☆ ☆

(A) 10

(B) 8

(C) 7

(D) 4

2

(A) △

(B) ▢

(C) ▭

(D) ◯

3

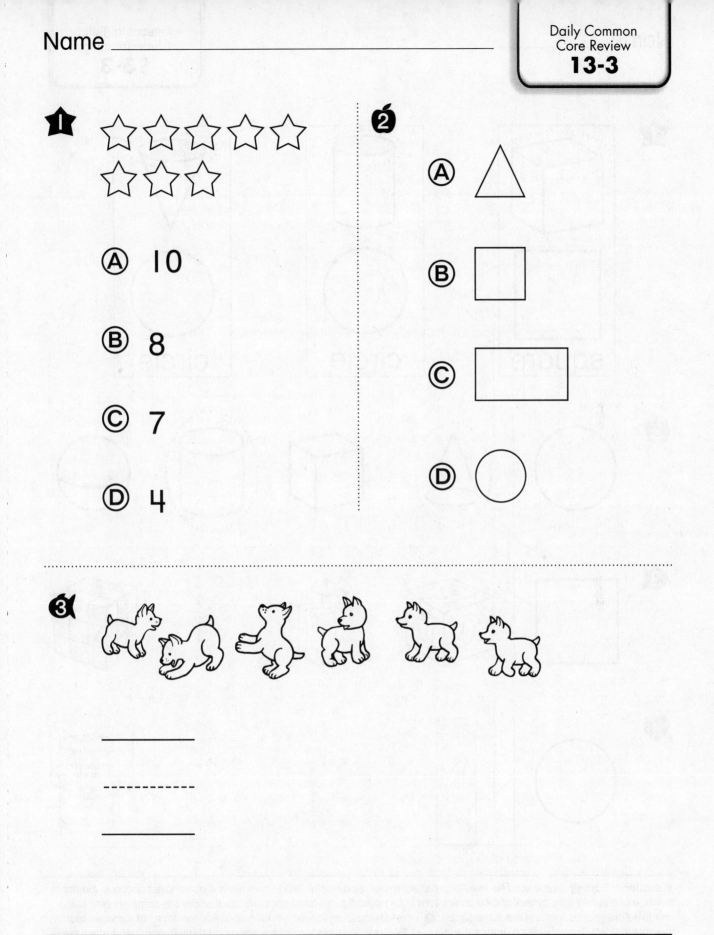

_____

- - - - - - - -

_____

Directions Have students: **1** mark the number that tells how many stars; **2** mark the triangle; **3** count the puppies, and then write the number that tells how many.

Name _____

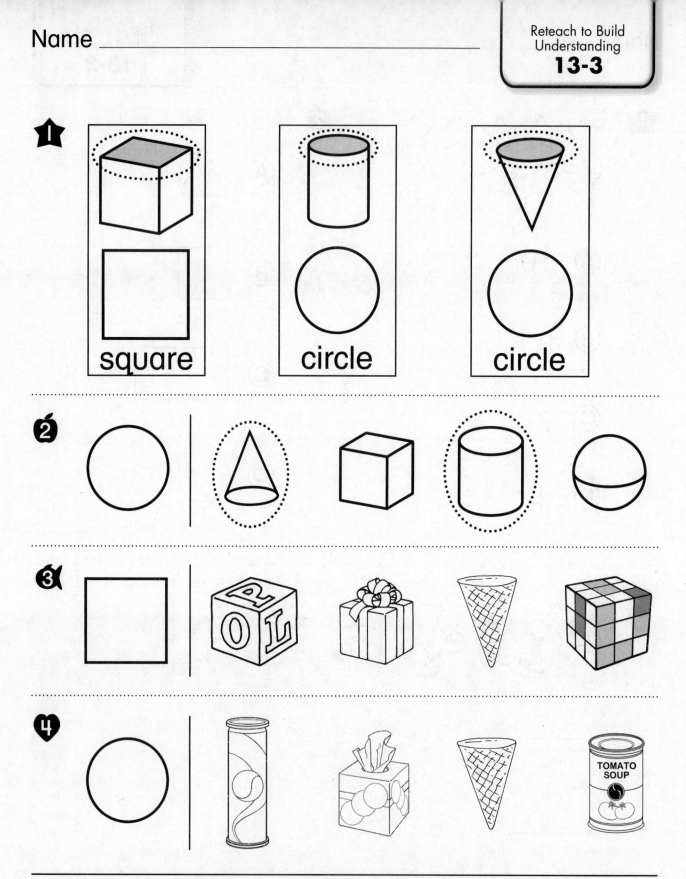

★ **1**

square   circle   circle

2

3

4

Directions Say: ★ *Some solid figures have* **flat surfaces**. *Spheres do* NOT *have flat surfaces. What shape is the flat surface of a cube? Of a cylinder? Of a cone? Which two solid figures have flat surfaces that are the same shape? Color the two flat surfaces that are the same shape;* ❷ *What shape is on the left? Which solid figures have flat surfaces that are this shape? Draw a circle around them.* ❸ *and* ❹ *Have students look at the shape on the left, and then draw a circle around the objects that have a flat surface with that shape.* **On the Back!** *Draw a square or a circle, and then name 2 different objects with a flat surface that matches that shape.*

⭐ **1**

Ⓐ

Ⓑ

Ⓒ

Ⓓ

🍎 **2**

Ⓐ 2

Ⓑ 3

Ⓒ 4

Ⓓ 5

🐟 **3**

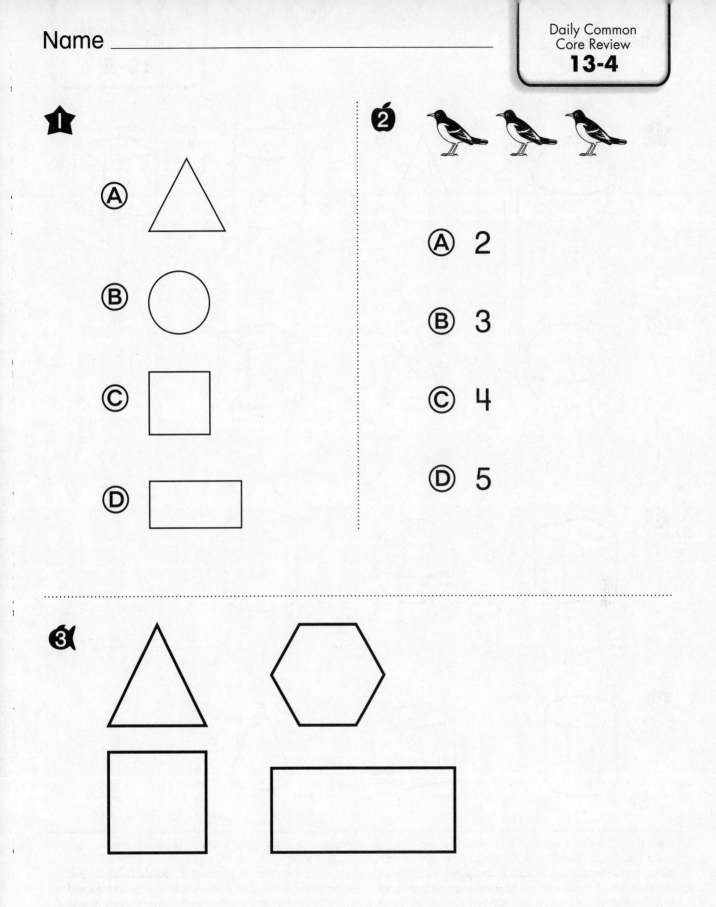

Directions Have students: ⭐ mark the circle; 🍎 mark the number that tells how many birds; 🐟 color the hexagon.

Name _____

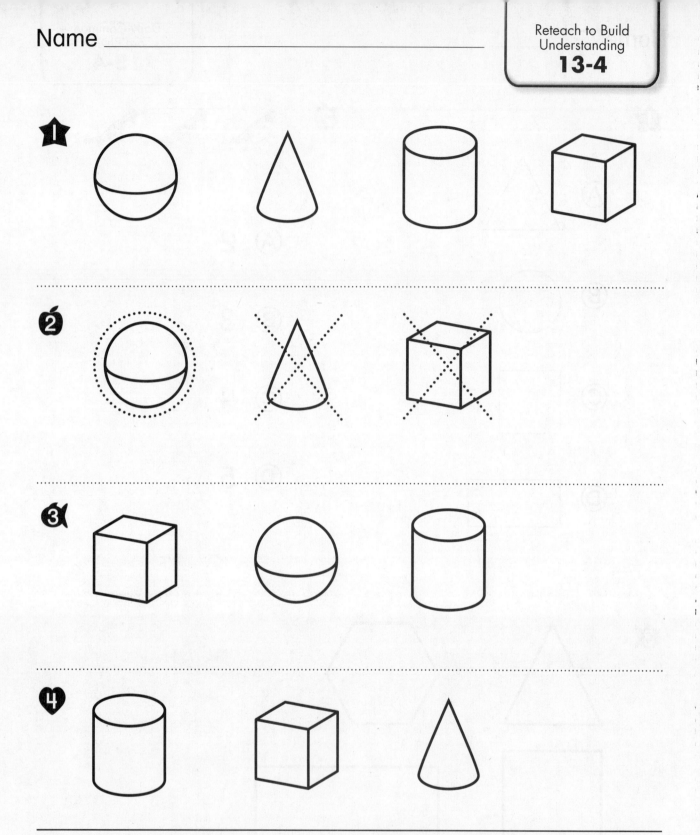

Directions Say: ⭐ *Let's say the names of these solid figures together: sphere, cone, cylinder, cube. Solid figures with a flat surface can* **stack**. *Which of these solid figures can stack? Draw a circle around them. Why can't a sphere stack?* 🍎 *Listen to these clues to find the shape that the clues describe. Clue 1: I can roll. Which shape does NOT roll? Mark an X on the cube. Clue 2: I do NOT have any flat surfaces. How many flat surfaces does a cone have? Since a cone has one flat surface, mark an X on it to show it does NOT match the clue. Which shape fits the clues? Draw a circle around it. Have students listen to the clues, mark Xs on the solid figures that do NOT fit the clues, and draw a circle around the solid figure the clues describe. Say:* ❸ *I can roll. I can also stack. Which shape am I?* ❹ *I can stack. I have more than two flat surfaces. Which shape am I? Explain which clues helped you solve the mystery.* **On the Back!** *Have students draw a cube, a sphere, a cone, or a cylinder. Then have them tell three clues that describe their solid figure.*

Play a Game

Start 👥 Get 14 red squares.

Put [1] [2] [3] [4] in a 🛍.

Player 1

Player 2

Materials   14 red squares, number tiles 1–4, paper bag

Oral Directions   **TRY** Choose a game board. Take turns. Pick a tile. If you pick a 1, cover a shape that rolls and has only 1 flat surface. If you pick a 2, cover a shape that rolls and has 2 flat surfaces. If you pick a 3, cover a shape that has 6 flat surfaces. If you pick a 4, cover a shape that has no flat surfaces. Put the tile back in the bag. The first player to cover all 7 game spaces wins.

TRY AGAIN If you have time, play again!

Center Game ★ 13·4

Play a Game

Start 👥 Get 18 red squares.
Get 20 blue squares.

IF THE FIGURES	COLLECT
Roll	◼
Roll and have flat surfaces	◼ ◼
Have flat surfaces and CANNOT roll	◼ ◼ ◼

Materials   18 red squares, 20 blue squares

Oral Directions   **TRY** Cover every game space with a red square. Take turns. On your turn, uncover one game space. Set the red square aside. If both solid figures roll, collect 1 blue square. If both solid figures roll and have flat surfaces, collect 2 blue squares. If both figures have flat surfaces and CANNOT roll, collect 3 blue squares. The first player to collect 10 blue squares wins.

TRY AGAIN If you have time, play again!

Name _____

1

Ⓐ (bird)

Ⓑ (butterfly)

Ⓒ (squirrel)

Ⓓ (bee)

2

Ⓐ 1

Ⓑ 2

Ⓒ 3

Ⓓ 4

3

$5 + 4 = 9$ $5 + 2 = 7$

$5 + 3 = 8$ $4 + 3 = 7$

Directions Have students: **1** mark the animal that is next to the tree; **2** mark the number that tells how many nests; **3** listen to the story, and then draw a circle around the equation that tells the story. Say: *There are 5 flowers. 2 more grow. How many flowers are there in all?*

Name _____

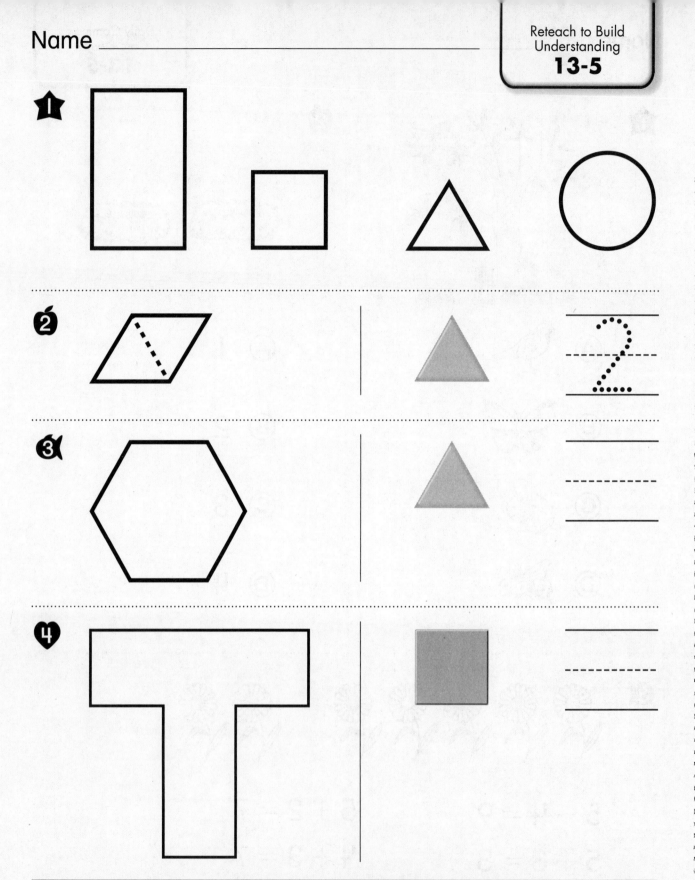

Directions Say: ⭐ *Let's say the names of these shapes together: rectangle, square, triangle, circle. Color the* **circle** *orange, the* **square** *blue, the* **rectangle** *green, and the* **triangle** *red;* 🍎 *Let's use triangle pattern blocks to cover the shape on the left. How many do you need to cover the shape? Draw a line to show how many blocks you used. Now write the number that tells how many.* 🌀 *and* 💛 *Have students use the pattern block shown to cover the shape, draw the lines, and then write the number that tells how many pattern blocks to use.* **On the Back!** *Have students use pattern blocks to create a picture, and then tell how many of each shape they used.*

Try Together

Start 👫 Put 4 5 6 7 8 in a 🛍.

Get 40 squares.

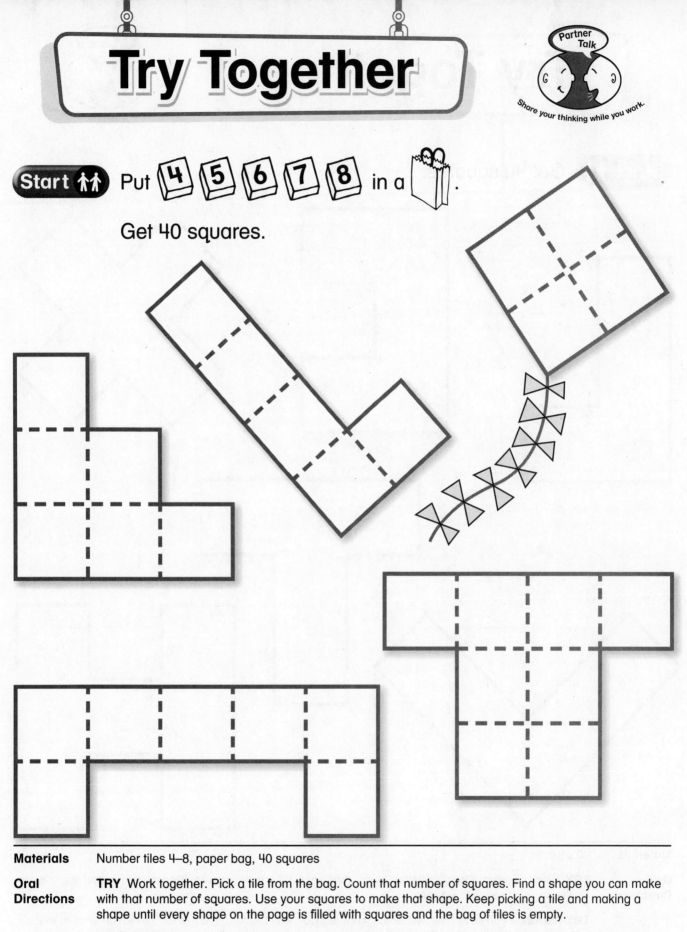

Materials   Number tiles 4–8, paper bag, 40 squares

Oral Directions   **TRY** Work together. Pick a tile from the bag. Count that number of squares. Find a shape you can make with that number of squares. Use your squares to make that shape. Keep picking a tile and making a shape until every shape on the page is filled with squares and the bag of tiles is empty.

TRY AGAIN If you have time, remove the squares from each shape one at a time. Count as you remove them. Point to a shape. Ask your partner to make that shape. Or, use squares to make your own shapes!

Try Together

Start 👥 Get 40 squares.

Materials   40 squares

Oral Directions   **TRY** Work together. Choose a letter. Name that letter. Fill it with squares. Work together until every letter on the page is filled with squares.

TRY AGAIN If you have time, tell which letter is made with the fewest squares. Tell which letter is made with the most squares. Tell which letters are made with the same number of squares. Then use squares to make other letters.

Name _____

1

Ⓐ [rectangle]

Ⓑ [square]

Ⓒ [vertical rectangle]

Ⓓ [hexagon]

2

Ⓐ [rectangle]

Ⓑ [triangle]

Ⓒ [hexagon]

Ⓓ [trapezoid]

3

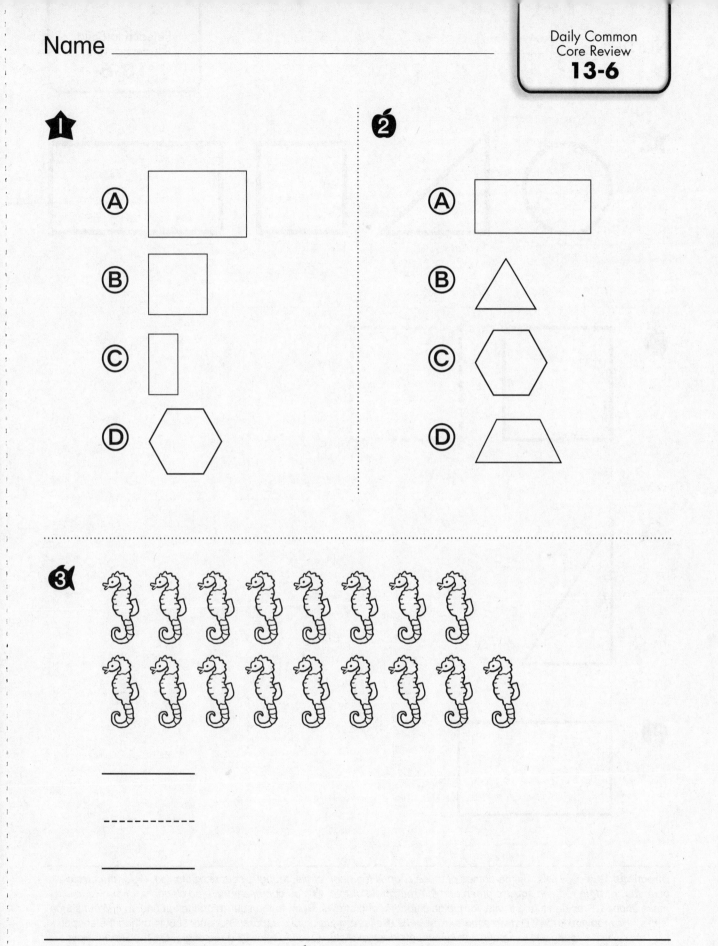

_____

- - - - - - - - - - -

_____

Directions Have students: **1** mark the square; **2** mark the rectangle; **3** count the seahorses, and then write the number that tells how many.

Name _____

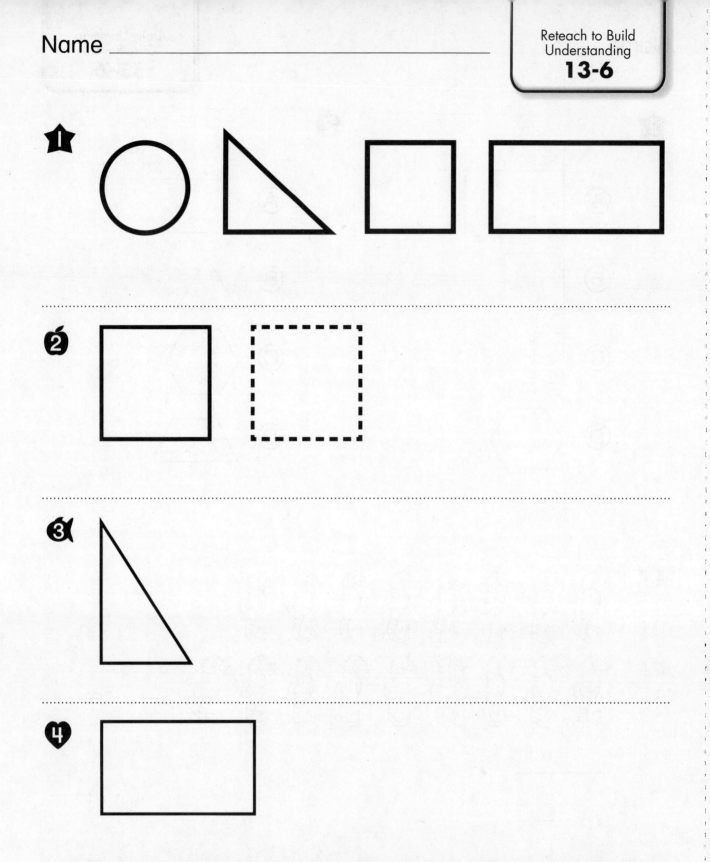

Directions Say: ★ *Let's say the names of these shapes together: circle, triangle, square, rectangle. Color the* **circle** *blue, the* **triangle** *red, the* **square** *green and the* **rectangle** *purple;* ② *You can use yarn, pipe cleaners, or straws to make shapes.* Provide students with yarn, pipe cleaners, and straws. Point to the square on the left and say: *What shape is this? How do you know? Draw a square. Now, let's use [straws] to build a square.* Students should attach the shapes they make with materials to this page. Have students draw or build: ③ a triangle; ④ a rectangle. **On the Back!** Have students use yarn, pipe cleaners, or straws to make a circle, attach it to the paper, and then explain why some materials are easier to use to make a circle than others.

Name _____

⭐ 1

Ⓐ

Ⓑ

Ⓒ

Ⓓ

🍎 2

Ⓐ ♡♡♡

Ⓑ ♡♡♡♡

Ⓒ ♡♡♡♡♡

Ⓓ ♡♡♡♡♡♡

⭐ 3

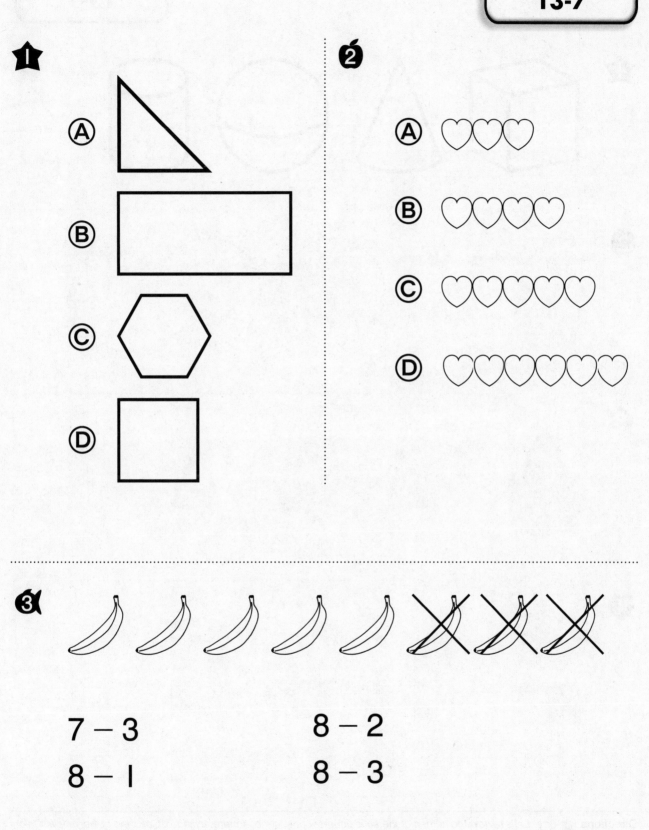

7 − 3   8 − 2

8 − 1   8 − 3

Directions Have students: ⭐ mark the triangle; 🍎 mark the picture that shows a group of 4 hearts; ⭐ draw a circle around the subtraction that tells about the bananas.

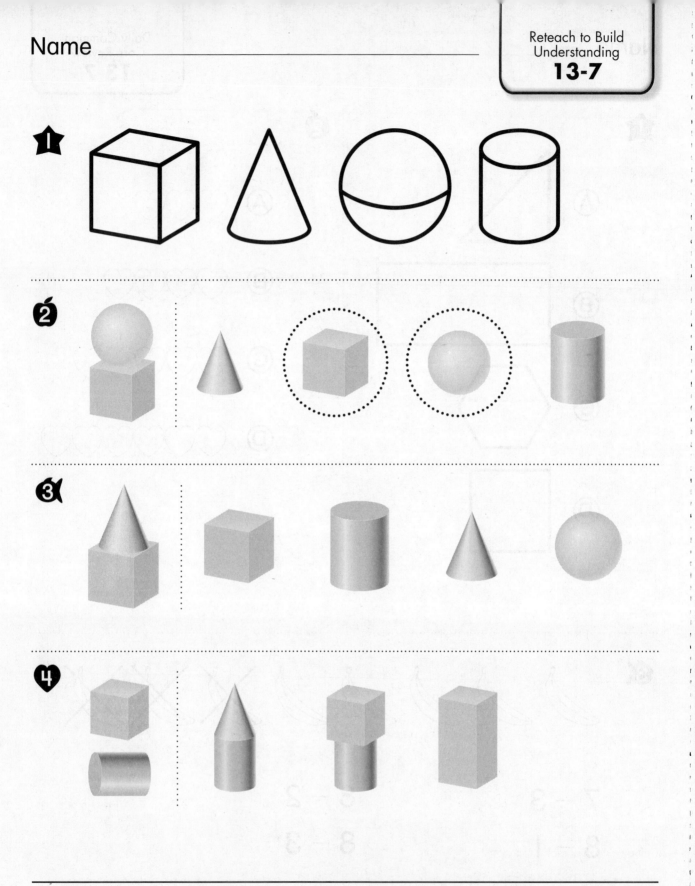

Directions ⭐ Say: *Let's review the names of the solid figures: cube, cone, sphere, cylinder. Color the **cube** yellow. Color the **cylinder** green. Color the **sphere** blue. Color the **cone** red.* Provide materials to build the solid figures. ② Point to the shape on the left. Say: *Which solid figures build this shape? Draw a circle around the solid figures on the right that can build this shape.* Have students use tools to: ③ build the shape on the left, and then draw a circle around the solid figures that can build the shape; ④ find the shape the solid figures can build, and then draw a circle around the shape. **On the Back!** Have students use materials to build a solid figure that is NOT a cube. Have a partner name the solid figure.

Play a Game

Start 👫 Put 1 2 3 4 5 6 in a 🛍.

Get 8 red squares.

PLAYER 1

PLAYER 2

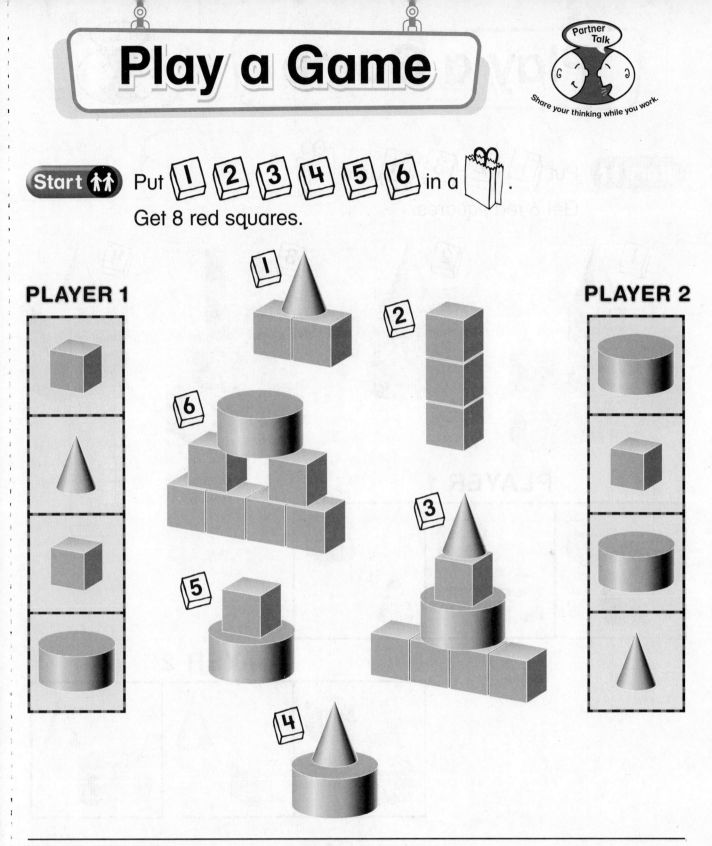

Materials	Number tiles 1–6, paper bag, 8 red squares
Oral Directions	**TRY** Tell why the solid figures in each tower can be stacked. Choose a game board. Take turns. Pick a number tile from the bag. Find the tower that is next to your number. If you see a solid figure in that tower on your game board, name the solid figure and cover it with a red square. If not, lose a turn. Put the tile back in the bag. The first player to cover all 4 solid figures on a game board wins.
	TRY AGAIN If you have more time, play again! This time, choose a different game board.

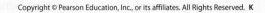

Play a Game

Start 👫 Put [1] [2] [3] [4] in a 🛍.

Get 6 red squares.

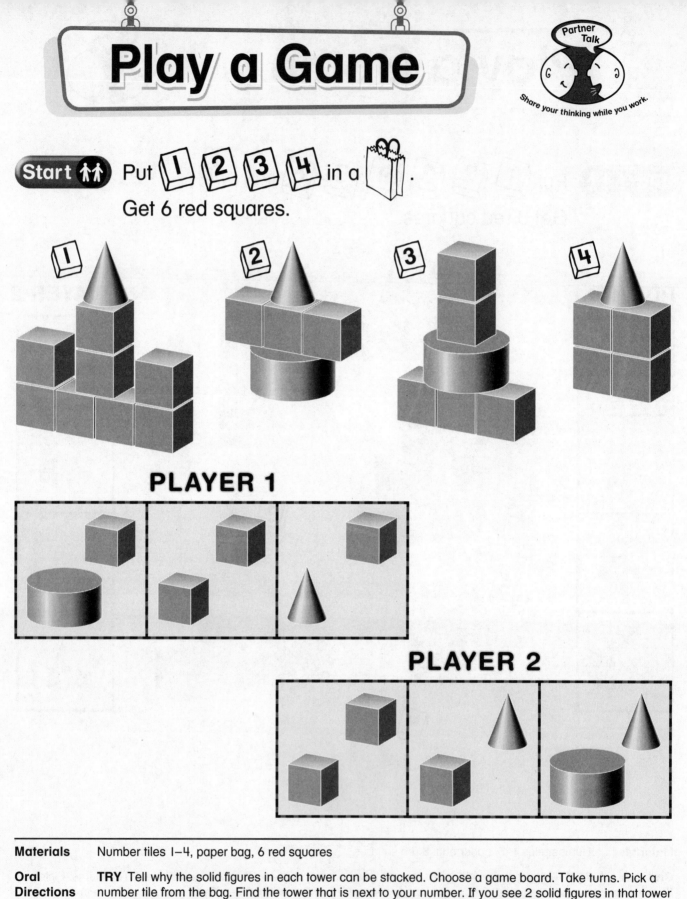

PLAYER 1

PLAYER 2

Materials   Number tiles 1–4, paper bag, 6 red squares

Oral Directions   **TRY** Tell why the solid figures in each tower can be stacked. Choose a game board. Take turns. Pick a number tile from the bag. Find the tower that is next to your number. If you see 2 solid figures in that tower on your game board, name both solid figures and cover those figures with a red square. If not, lose a turn. Put the tile back in the bag. The first player to cover all 3 game spaces on a game board wins.

TRY AGAIN If you have more time, play again! This time, choose a different game board.

This book belongs to:

When Bob Shops

Written by Carolyn Fleck   Illustrated by Jenny B. Harris

Bob wants the biggest bear. Which bear does Bob buy?

fold down

Bob wants the largest umbrella. Which one will he buy?

Bob buy?

Which shirt does

a smaller size.

Bob needs

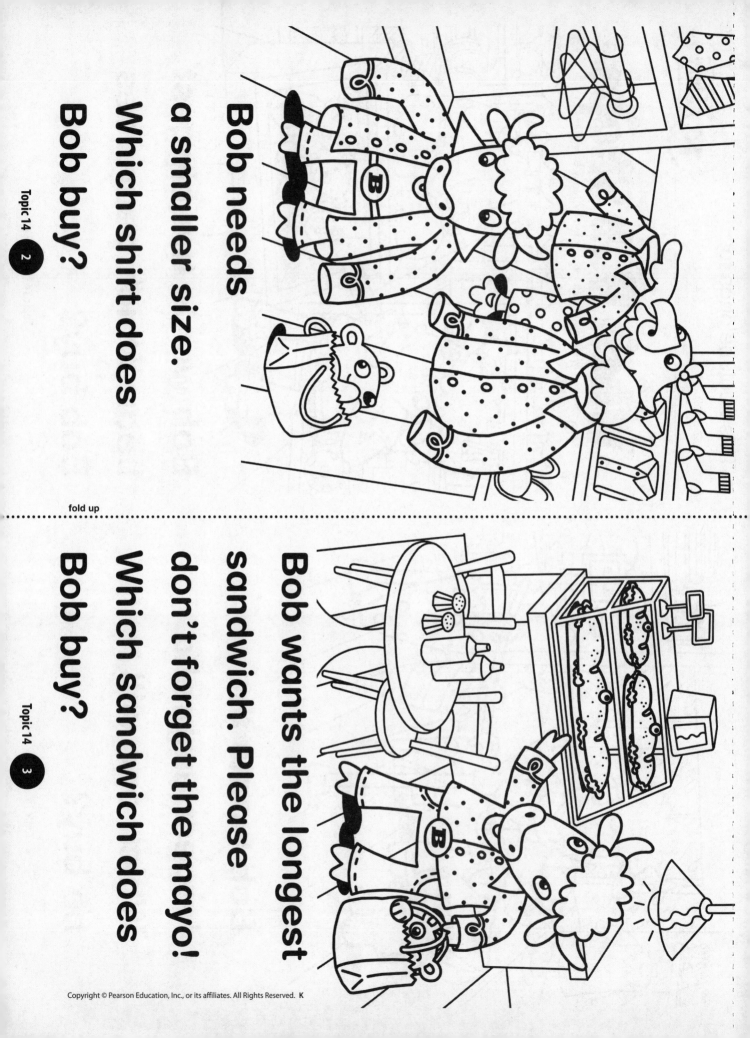

fold up

Bob buy?

Which sandwich does

don't forget the mayo!

sandwich. Please

Bob wants the longest

Name _____

Describe and Compare Measurable Attributes

Topic 14 Standards
K.MD.A.1, K.MD.A.2
See the front of the Student's Edition for complete standards.

Dear Family,

Your child is learning to use measurement to describe and compare different objects. In this topic, he or she will learn to compare objects based on length, height, weight, and capacity.

Measure
Objects can be measured and described by their attributes.

Here is an activity to do with your child to practice measurement.

Is it Longer?

Give your child a pencil. Have him or her find an object in your home that is longer than the pencil. Then have your child find an object in your home that is shorter than the pencil. Continue with other objects.

Observe Your Child

Focus on Mathematical Practice 3
Construct viable arguments and critique the reasoning of others.

Help your child become proficient with Mathematical Practice 3. After your child decides which object is longer, ask how he or she knows that the object is longer.

Describir y comparar atributos medibles

Estándares del Tema 14

K.MD.A.1, K.MD.A.2

Los estándares completos se encuentran en las páginas preliminares del Libro del estudiante.

Estimada familia:

Su niño(a) está aprendiendo a usar la medición para describir y comparar figuras geométricas. En este tema, aprenderá a comparar figuras según su longitud, altura, peso y capacidad.

Medir

Los objetos se pueden medir y describir según sus atributos.

Aquí se presenta una actividad que puede hacer con su niño(a) para practicar la medición.

¿Es más largo?

Dé a su niño(a) un lápiz. Pídale que halle un objeto en la casa que sea más largo que el lápiz y luego, que halle un objeto en la casa que sea más corto que el lápiz. Continúen con otros objetos.

Observe a su niño(a)

Enfoque en la Práctica matemática 3:

Construir argumentos viables y evaluar el razonamiento de otros.

Ayude a su niño(a) a adquirir competencia en la Práctica matemática 3. Después de que su niño(a) decida qué objeto es más largo, pídale que explique cómo lo sabe.

Name _____

Tools to Measure

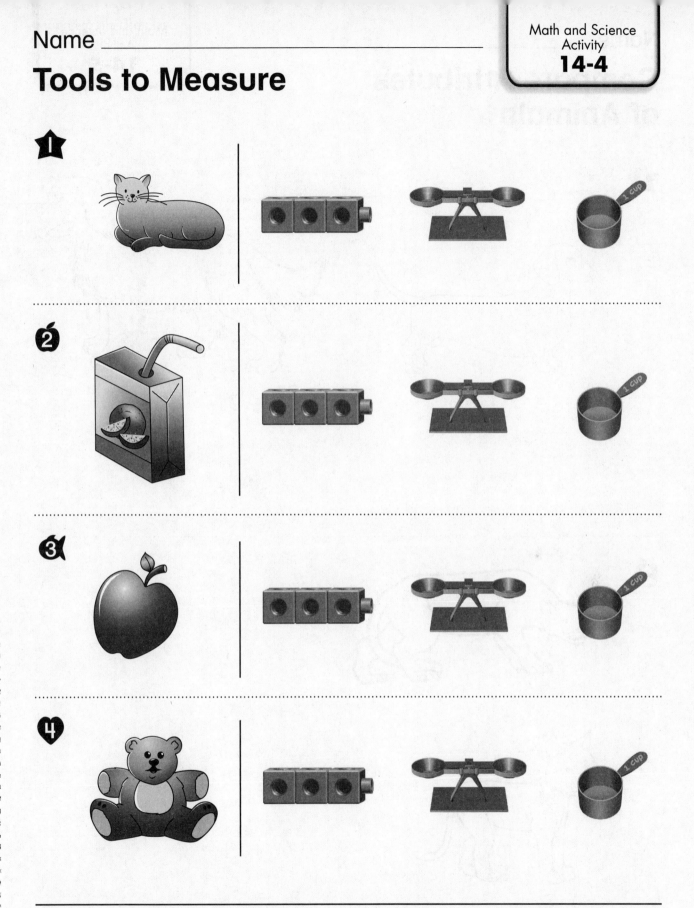

Name _____

Compare Attributes of Animals

1

2

Directions Say: *Did you know that scientists compare the attributes of animals in order to learn more about them?* Have students: **1** draw a circle around the dog that is taller; **2** draw a circle around the cat that is longer. **Extension** Have students draw 2 animals with different heights and 2 animals with different lengths.

⭐**1**

| 4 | 5 | 6 | ? | 8 |

Ⓐ 9

Ⓑ 7

Ⓒ 6

Ⓓ 0

🍎**2**   ◯ ◯ ◯ ⊗ ⊗

Ⓐ $5 - 2 = 3$ Ⓒ $5 - 4 = 1$

Ⓑ $5 - 3 = 2$ Ⓓ $5 - 5 = 0$

⭐**3**

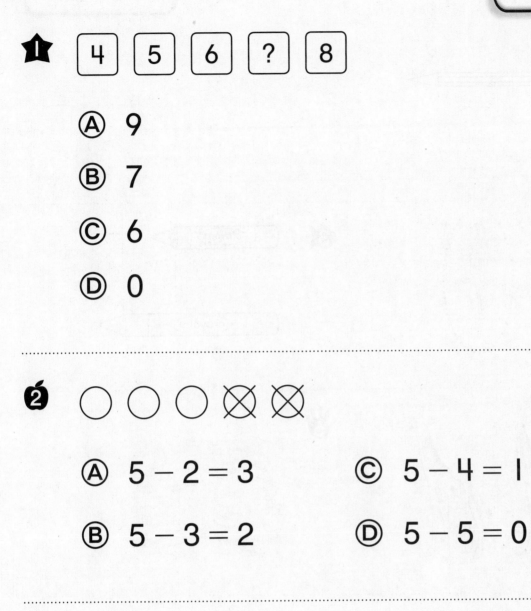

Directions Have students: ⭐ mark the missing number; 🍎 mark the equation that matches the picture; ⭐ look at the shape on the left, and then draw a circle around all the solid figures that have a flat surface with that same shape.

Name _____

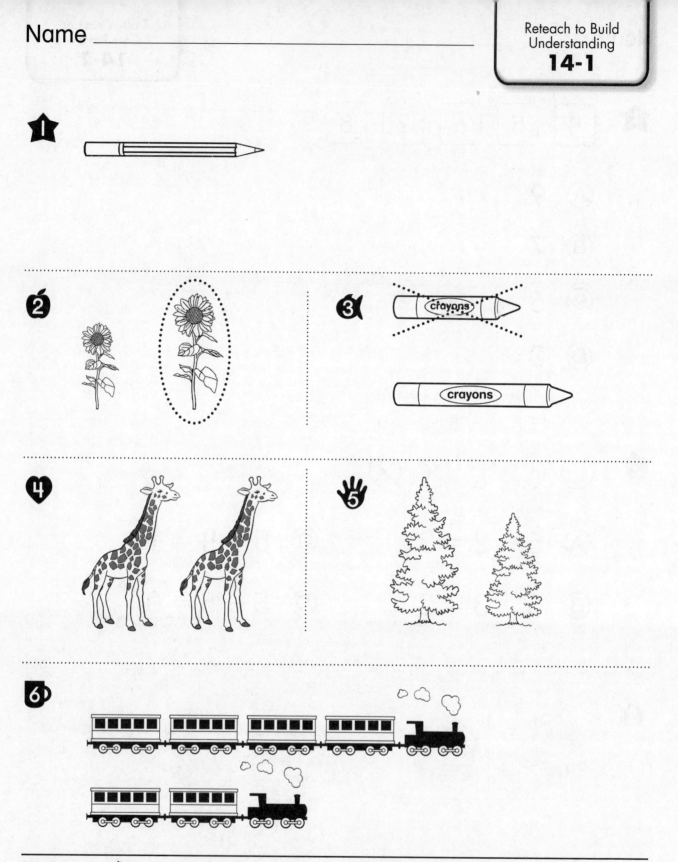

Directions Say: ⭐ *You can use the words* same, shorter, *and* longer *to* **compare** *the lengths of objects. Draw a pencil that is longer than the pencil shown.* ② *You can use the words* same, shorter, *and* taller *to compare the heights of objects. Look at the flowers. Which flower is taller? Draw a circle around it. Point to the other flower. This flower is shorter.* Have students: ③ mark an X on the shorter crayon or underline both crayons if they are the same length; ④ and ✋ draw a circle around the taller object or underline both objects if they are the same height; ⑥ mark an X on the shorter train or underline both trains if they are the same length. **On the Back!** Have students draw a worm and then draw another worm that is shorter than the first worm they drew.

Name _____

⭐ 1

Ⓐ ◯

Ⓑ △

Ⓒ ▢

Ⓓ ▢

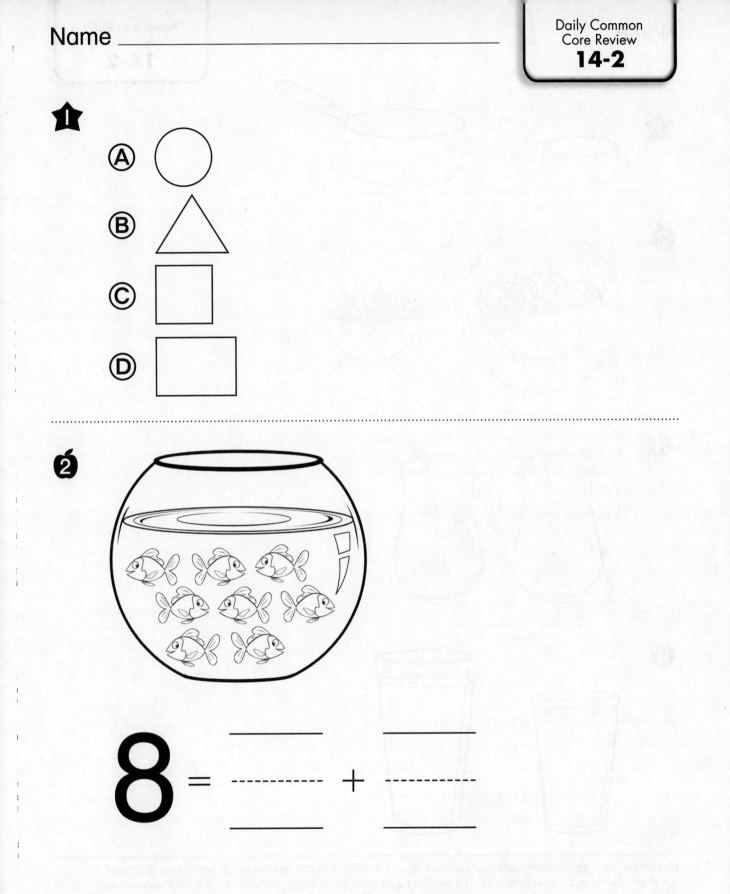

🍎 2

$$8 = \underline{\qquad} + \underline{\qquad}$$

Directions Have students: ⭐ mark the square; 🍎 draw a circle around 2 groups of fish to show a number pair for 8, and then complete the equation to show the number pair.

Name _____

Directions Say: ⭐ *Capacity tells how much an object can hold. You can use the words* same, less, *and* more *to compare how much an object can hold. The pot that holds more has a larger capacity than the pot that holds less. Look at the 2 pots. Color the pot that holds more than the other pot;* 🍎 *Look at the 2 bowls. Which bowl holds more than the other bowl? Draw a circle around it. Which bowl holds less? Mark an X on it.* 🐟 *and* 🐸 *Have students draw a circle around the container that holds more and mark an X on the container that holds less, or underline both containers if they hold the same amount.* **On the Back!** *Have students draw a cup, and then draw another cup that holds more than the first one they drew.*

Look and See

Start Put 1 2 3 4 5 6 in a .

Get 6 red squares. Get 6 blue squares.

Materials	Number tiles 1–6, a bag for the tiles, 6 red squares, 6 blue squares
Oral Directions	**TRY** Take turns. Pick a number tile from the bag. Look at the 2 pictures next to that number. Tell where you have seen these things. Tell which object holds more. Put a blue square below it. Tell which object holds less. Put a red square below it. Take turns until the bag is empty.
	TRY AGAIN If you have time, begin again! If you have more time, name things that would hold more than a pail. Ask your partner to name things that would hold less than a pail.

Look and See

Start Put 1 2 3 4 5 6 in a .

Materials Number tiles 1–6, a bag for the tiles

Oral Directions **TRY** Take turns. Pick a tile from the bag. Look at the picture next to that number. Talk about what you see in the picture. Name something that holds less than what you see in the picture. Let your partner name something that holds more. Take turns until the bag is empty.

TRY AGAIN If you have time, begin again! If you have more time, name 2 objects you have at home. Tell your partner which one holds more. Tell your partner which one holds less.

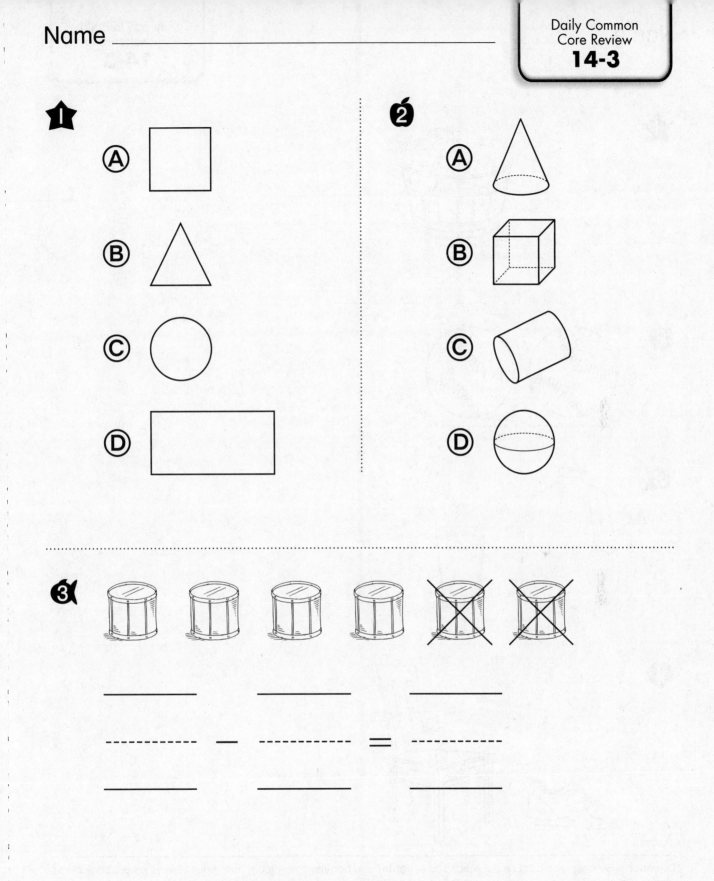

1

Ⓐ

Ⓑ

Ⓒ

Ⓓ

2

Ⓐ

Ⓑ

Ⓒ

Ⓓ

3

_____   _____   _____

---------- — ---------- = ----------

_____   _____   _____

Directions Have students: **1** mark the circle; **2** listen to the clues, and then mark the shape that the clues describe.
Say: *I have more than I flat surface. I can stack on top of another shape. I CANNOT roll. What solid figure am I?*
3 write an equation that matches the picture.

Name _____

1

2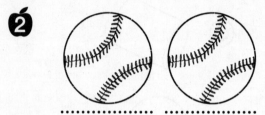

3

4

Directions Say: **1** *You can use the words same,* **lighter** *and* **heavier** *to compare how much objects weigh. Look at the apples. Do you think 1 apple is heavier or lighter than a basket of apples? Draw a circle around the object that is heavier. Mark an X on the object that is lighter;* **2** *Look at the baseballs. Is one baseball taller than the other? The baseballs are the same size and the same weight. Underline both baseballs to show that they weigh the same amount.* **3** *and* **4** Have students draw a circle around the heavier object and mark an X on the lighter object, or underline both objects if they are the same weight. **On the Back!** Have students draw 2 objects in the classroom, and then draw a circle around the lighter object.

Name _____

1

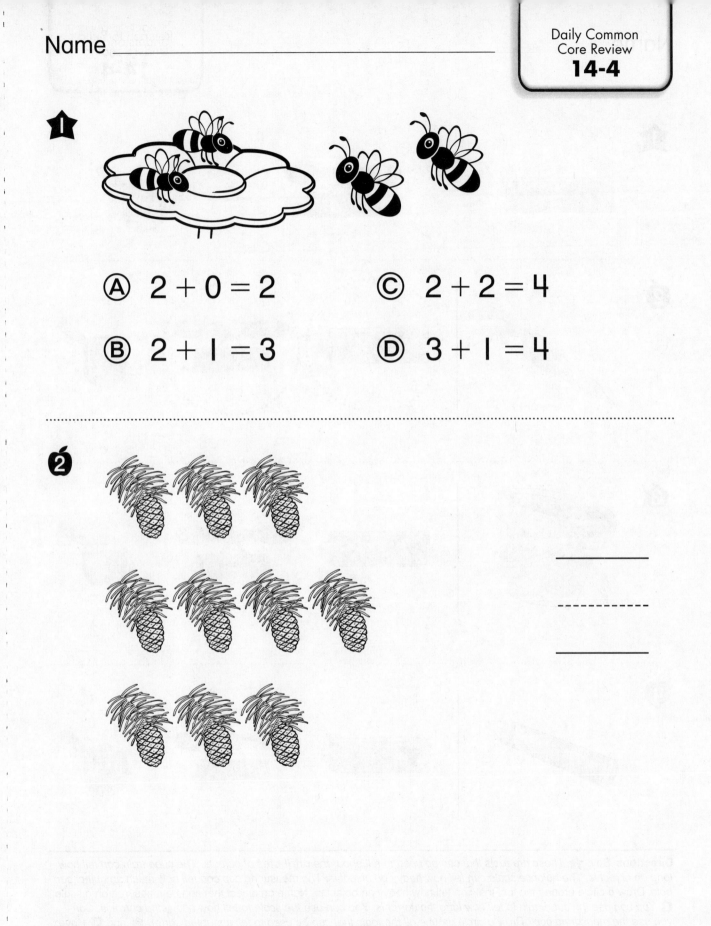

Ⓐ $2 + 0 = 2$ Ⓒ $2 + 2 = 4$

Ⓑ $2 + 1 = 3$ Ⓓ $3 + 1 = 4$

2

_____

- - - - - - - -

_____

Directions Have students: **1** mark the equation that tells how many; **2** count the pine cones, and then write the number that tells how many.

Name _____

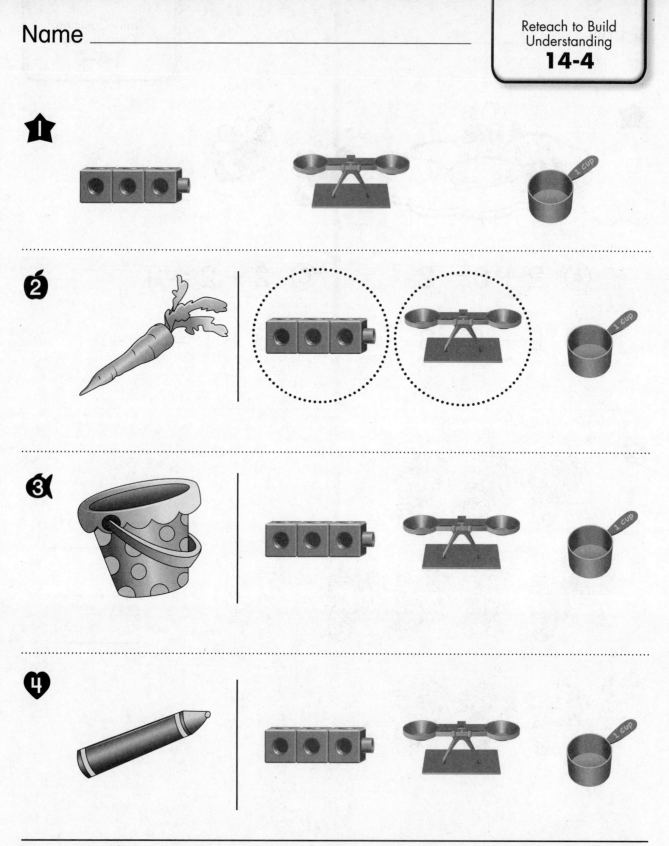

Directions Say: ⭐ *These are tools that can be used to tell about the **attributes** of objects. The cube train can tell how long an object is. The balance scale can tell how heavy an object is. The measuring cup can tell how much an object can hold.* Draw a circle around the tool that can tell how heavy an object is. Name an object that can be measured on a scale; 🍎 *You can use the cube train to tell how long the carrot is. You can use the scale to tell how heavy the carrot is. Can you use the measuring cup? Draw a circle around all the tools that can be used to tell about the carrot.* ❸ and ❹ Have students look at the object on the left, identify the attributes that can be measured, and then draw a circle around all the tools that could be used to tell about those attributes. **On the Back!** Draw an object, and then name all of the tools that could be used to tell about its attributes.

Name _____

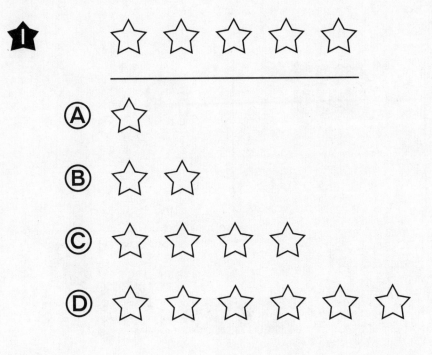

1 ☆ ☆ ☆ ☆ ☆
─────────────

Ⓐ ☆

Ⓑ ☆ ☆

Ⓒ ☆ ☆ ☆ ☆

Ⓓ ☆ ☆ ☆ ☆ ☆ ☆

2

 MARKER

─────────────

Directions Have students: **1** mark the group that has more stars than the group of stars at the top; **2** draw a circle around the writing tool that is longer than the marker at the top.

 D 14·5

Name _____

1

2

3

4

Directions Say: **1** *These are tools that can be used to tell about the **attributes** of objects. The cube train can tell how long an object is. The balance scale can tell how heavy an object is. The measuring cup can tell how much an object can hold. Draw an object that can be measured by each of the tools;* **2** *Look at the bowl. What attributes can be measured with the measuring cup? What about the cube train? Can you use the color wheel to measure attributes? Why or why not? Draw a circle around the measuring tools that could be used to tell about the attributes that can be measured.* **3** *and* **4** Have students look at the object on the left and identify the attributes that can be measured. Then have them draw a circle around the tools(s) that could be used to tell about those attributes and mark an X on the tool(s) that could NOT. **On the Back!** Have students draw an object in their home. Have them identify the attributes that can be measured, and then tell which measuring tools could be used to tell about the attributes that can be measured.

1

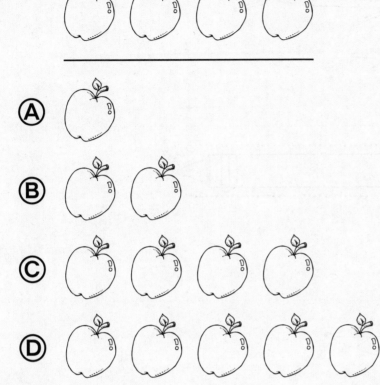

2

 |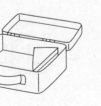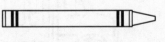

Directions Have students: **1** mark the group of apples that is equal in number to the group of apples at the top; **2** draw a circle around the object that is lighter than the apple.

 D 14·6

Copyright © Pearson Education, Inc., or its affiliates. All Rights Reserved. **K**

Name _____

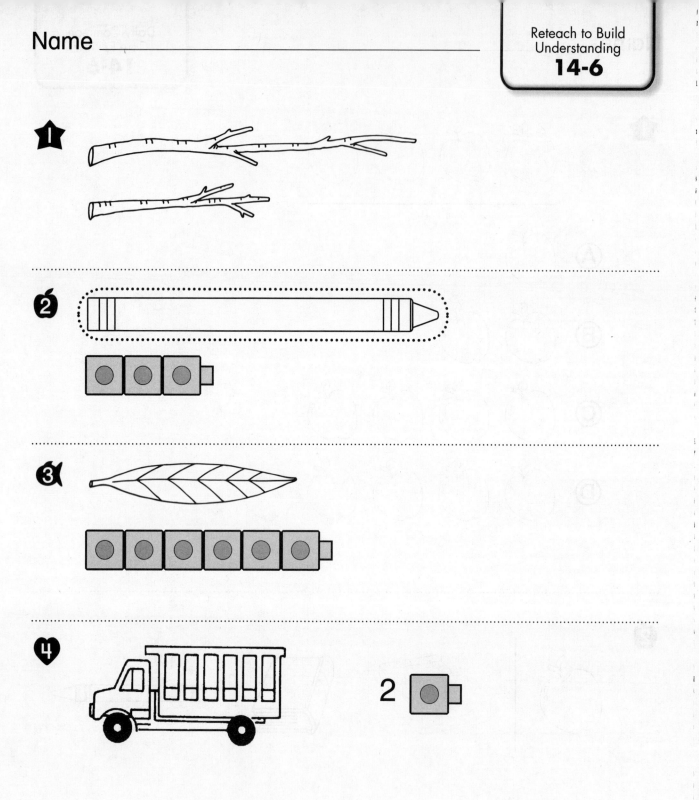

1

2

3

4

2

Directions Say: **1** *You can use the words* **longer** *and* **shorter** *to compare the lengths of objects. Which stick is longer? Draw a circle around it. Point to the other stick. This stick is shorter;* **2** *Look at the cube train. How many cubes are there? Compare the cube train and the crayon. Which one is longer? Draw a circle around it;* **3** *Compare the cube train and the leaf. Draw a circle around the one that is longer;* **4** *Make a cube train with the number of cubes shown, compare the length of the cube train to the toy truck, and then draw a circle around the one that is longer.* **On the Back!** *Have students draw a pencil and make a cube train with 3 cubes. Then ask students whether the cube train is longer or shorter than the pencil they drew.*

Play a Game

Start 👫 Put 1 2 3 4 in a 🛍.

Get 10 connecting cubes.
Get 20 red squares.

Player 1

ABC ABC ABC ABC ABC ABC ABC 2

♡ ♡ ♡ ♡ ♡ ♡ ♡ ♡ ♡ ♡ ♡ ♡ 3

Player 2

Materials	Number tiles 1–4, paper bag, 10 connecting cubes, 20 red squares
Oral Directions	**TRY** Decide who will be Player 1 and who will be Player 2. Find the game space where you will collect your red squares. Take turns. First use the cubes to make a cube train that is about the same length as the ribbon next to the scissors. Pick a number tile. Put your number tile on the ribbon next to that number. Check to see if the ribbon with the number is longer or shorter than the cube train. If the ribbon with the number is longer, get 2 red squares. If it is shorter, get 1 red square. Put the tile back in the bag. The first player to collect 8 squares wins.
	TRY AGAIN If you have more time, play again!

Play a Game

Partner Talk

Share your thinking while you work.

Start 👫 Put ⬜1 ⬜2 ⬜3 ⬜4 ⬜5 ⬜6 in a 🛍️.

Get 30 red or blue squares.

Player 1

Player 2

Materials   Number tiles 1–6, paper bag, 30 red or blue squares

Oral Directions   **TRY** Decide who will be Player 1 and who will be Player 2. Find the game space where you will collect your squares. Take turns. Pick a number tile. Put your number tile on the ribbon next to that number. Look for the ribbons that are longer than yours. If there is one ribbon that is longer, collect 1 square. If there are 2 ribbons, collect 2 squares. If there are 3 ribbons, collect 3 squares. If there are 4 ribbons that are longer, collect 4 squares. If there are 5 ribbons that are longer, collect 5 squares. If you cannot find any ribbons that are longer than yours, your turn ends. Put your tile back in the bag. The first player to collect 15 squares wins.

TRY AGAIN If you have more time, play again!

Name _____

Problem Solving Recording Sheet

Problem:

MAKE SENSE OF THE PROBLEM

Need to Find

Given

PERSEVERE IN SOLVING THE PROBLEM

Some Ways to Represent Problems
☐ Draw a Picture
☐ Write an Equation

Some Math Tools
☐ Objects
☐ Technology
☐ Paper and Pencil

Solution and Answer

CHECK THE ANSWER

Student Progress Report

Date _____

Dear Family,

Your child has just completed Topic _____ in our math program.

Teacher Comments:

_____

_____

_____

_____

_____

_____

- ✂

Name of student: _____

I have received and reviewed this progress report for my child.

_____

Parent/Guardian Signature

Parent/Guardian Comments:

_____

_____

_____

Name _____

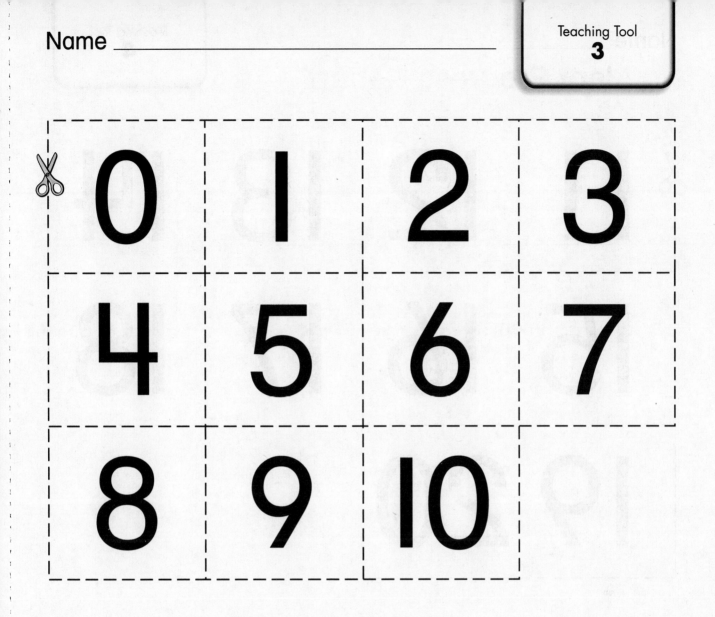

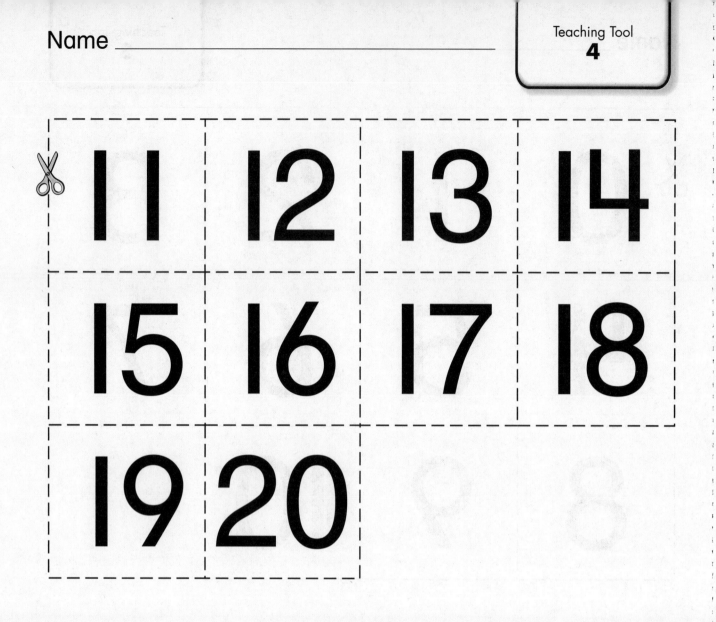

Name _____

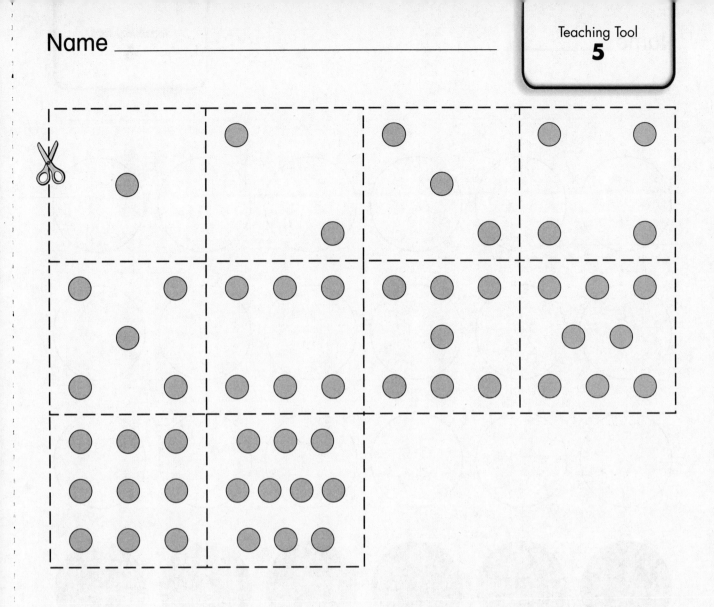

Name _____

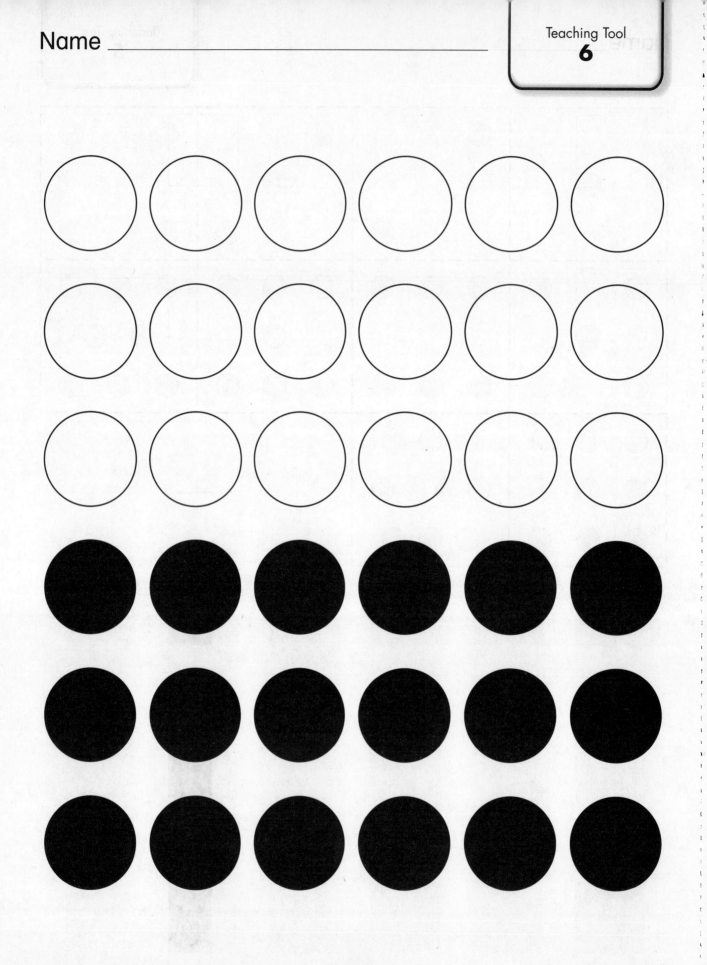

Two-Color Counters 6

Name _____

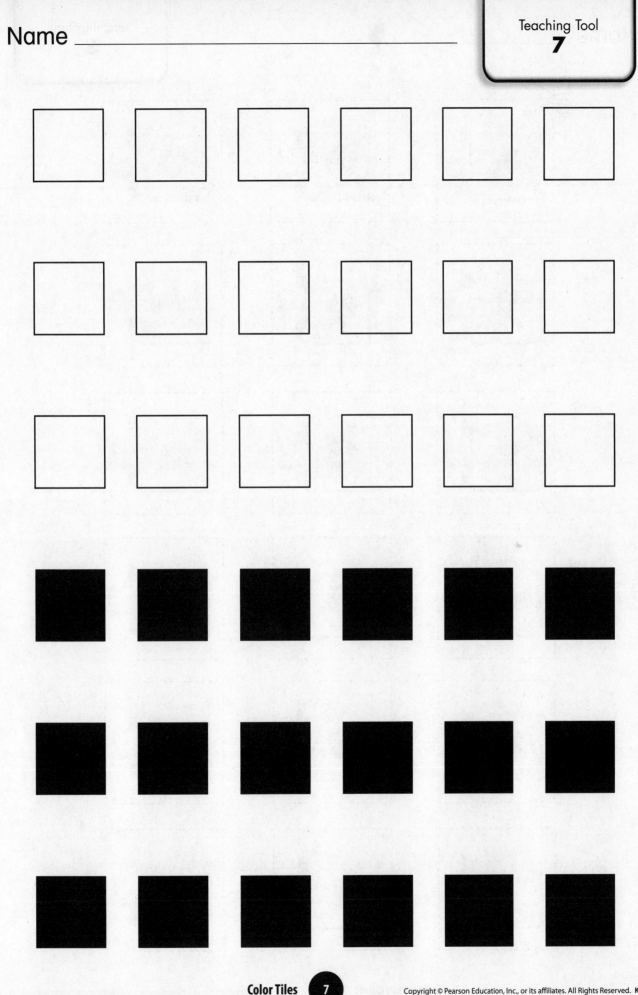

Name _____

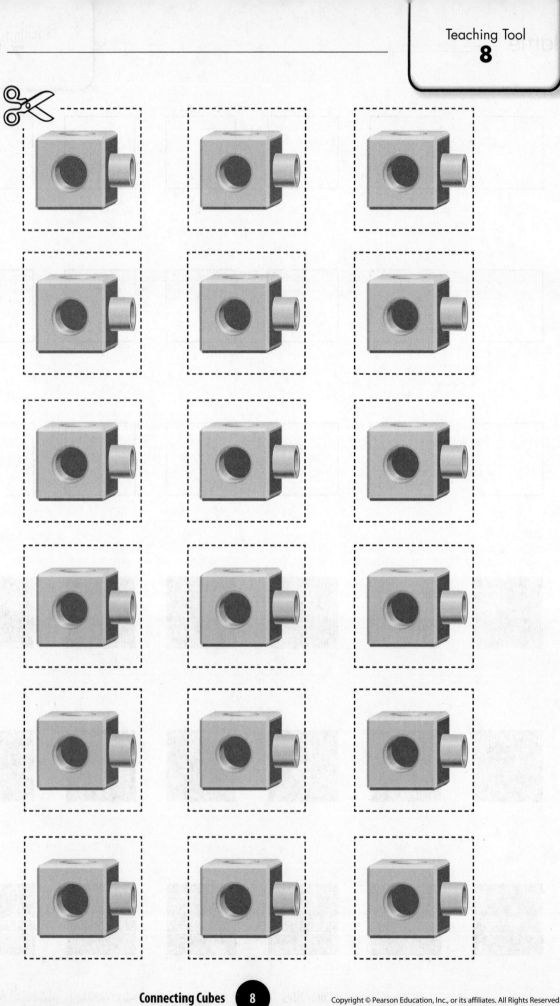

Name _____

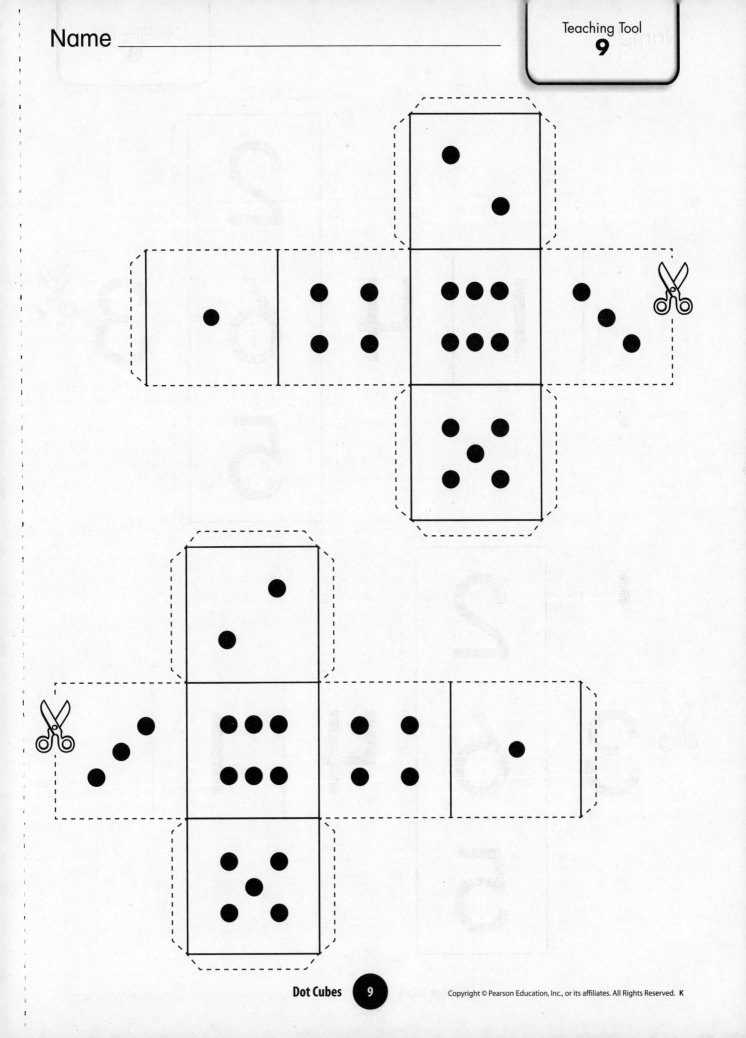

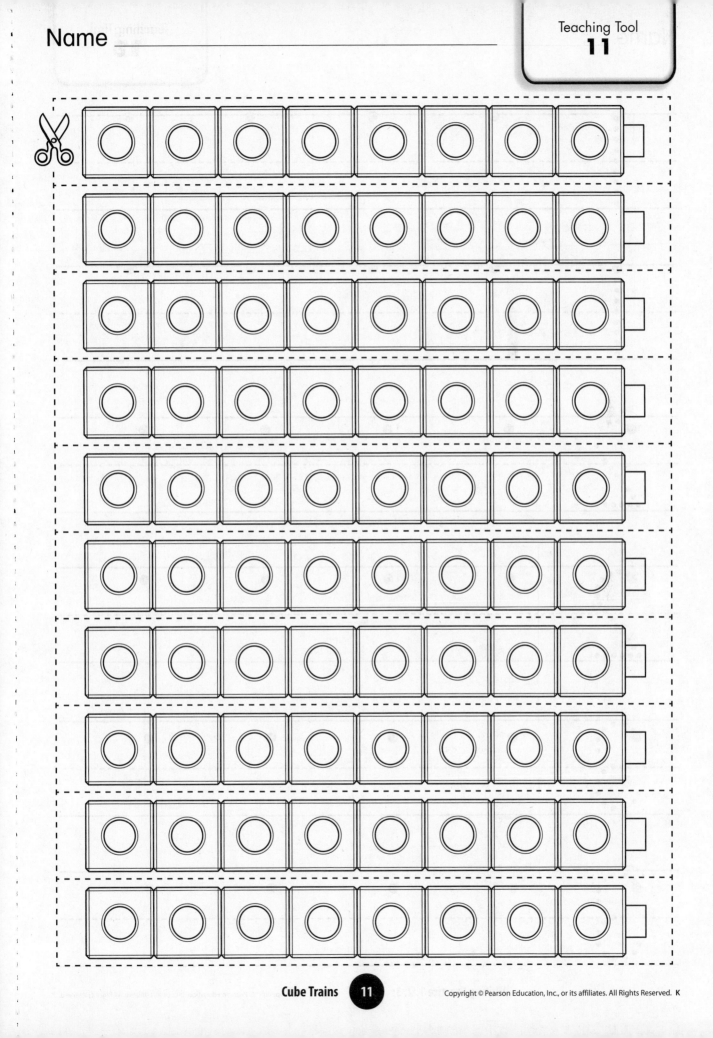

Name _____

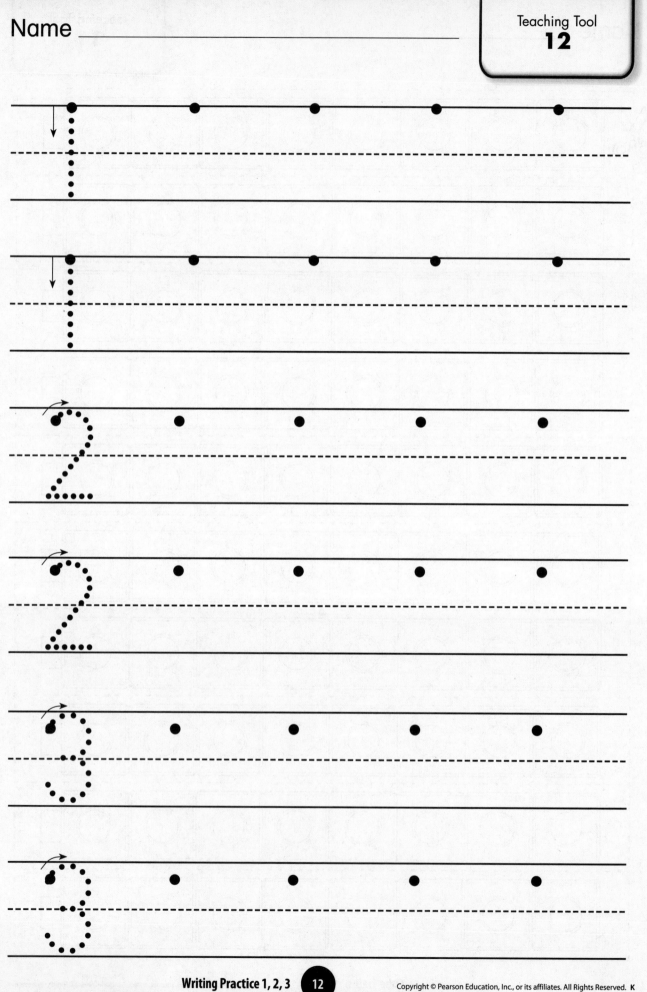

Name _____

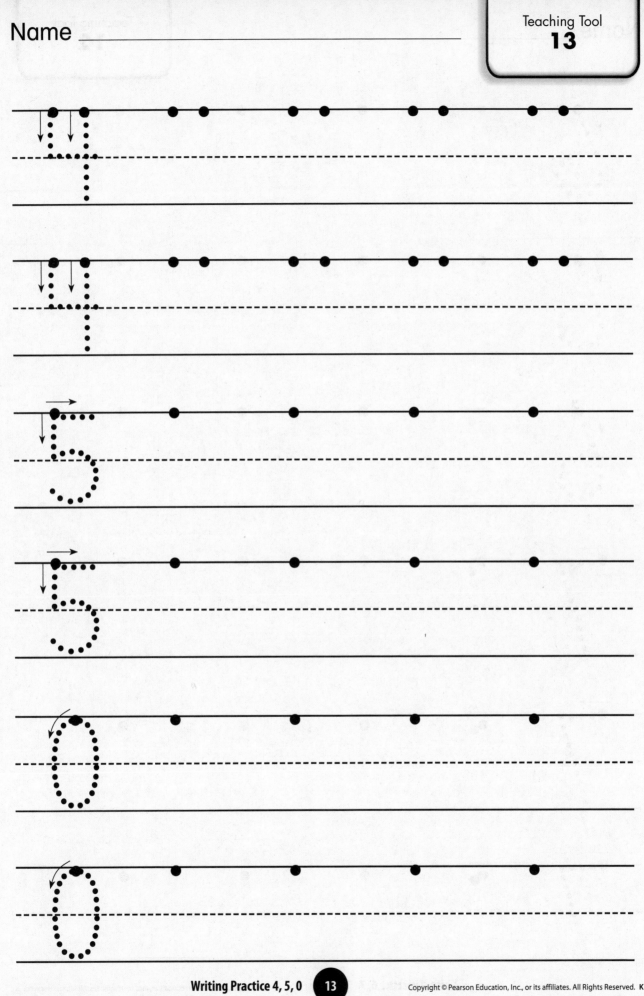

Name _____

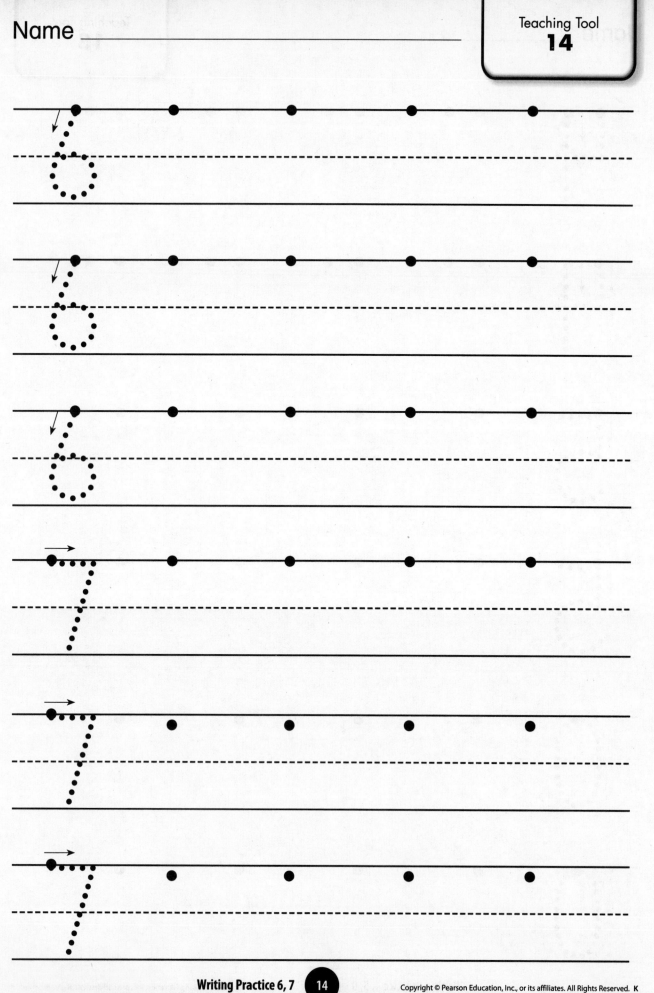

Name _____

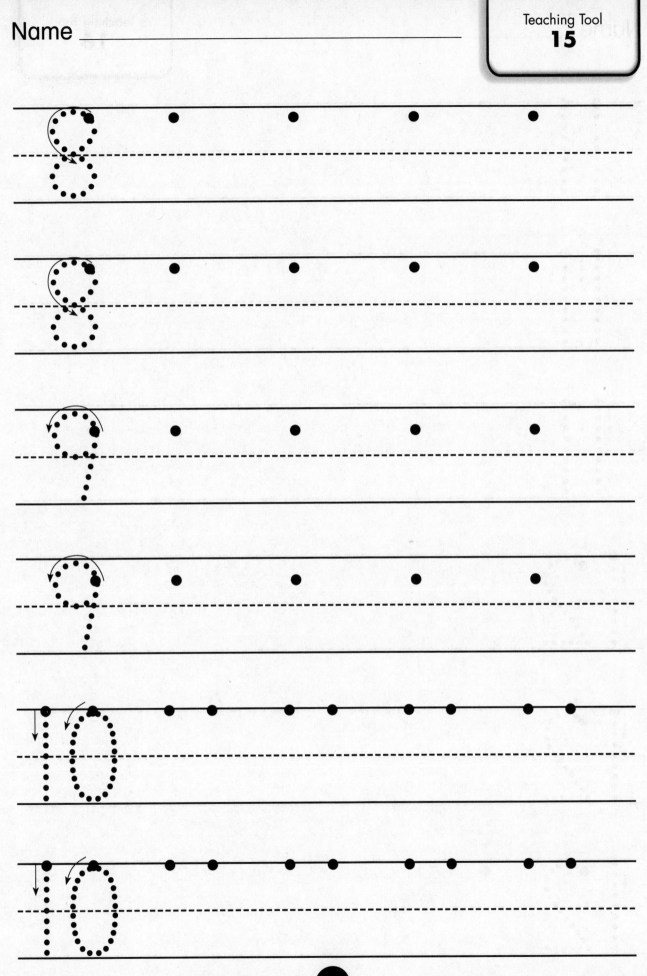

Name _____

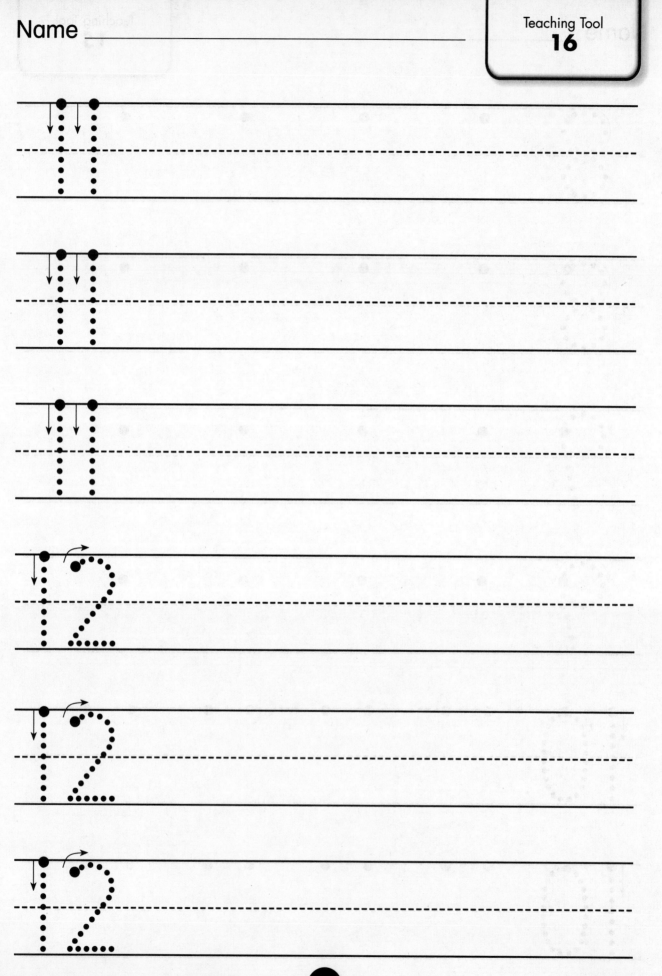

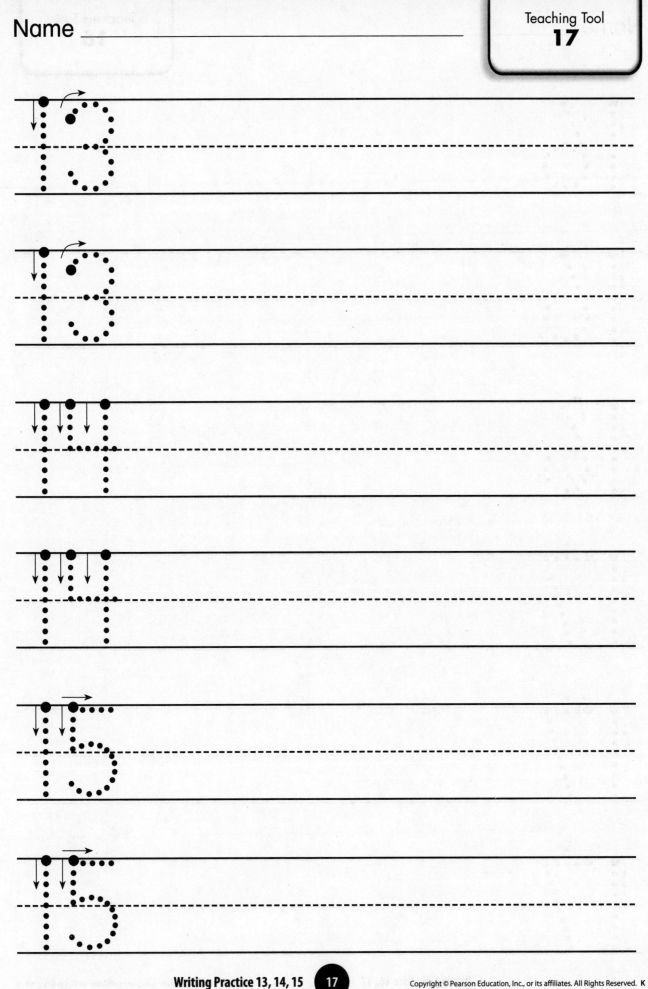

Name _____

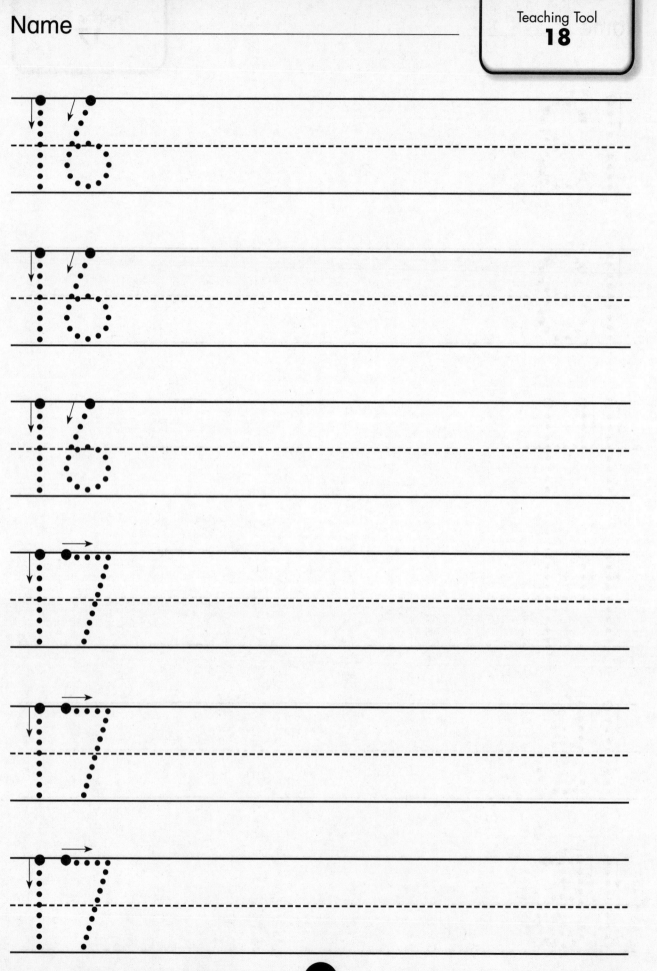

Name _____

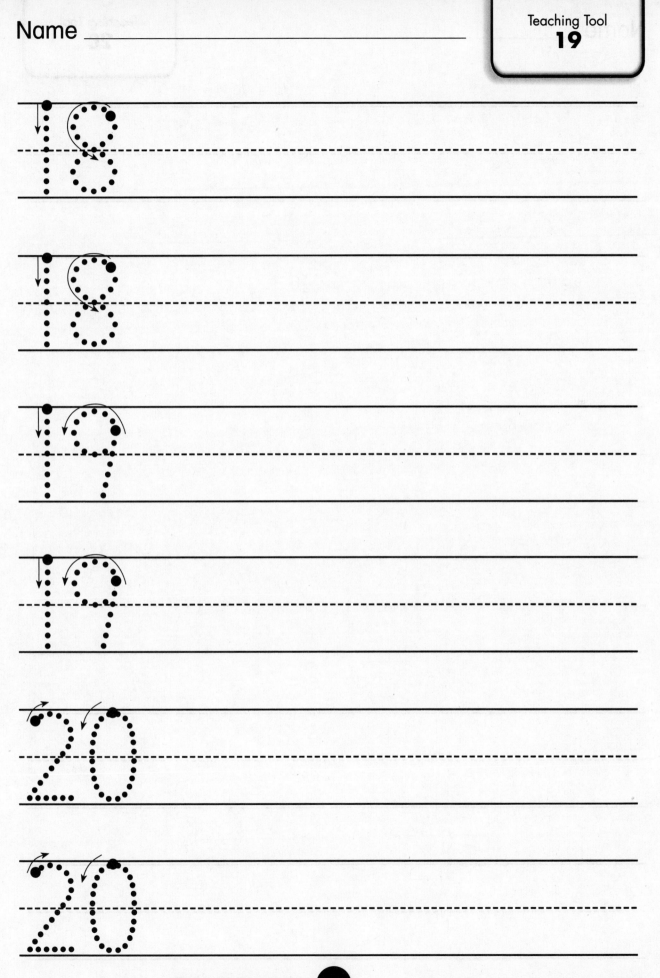

Name _____

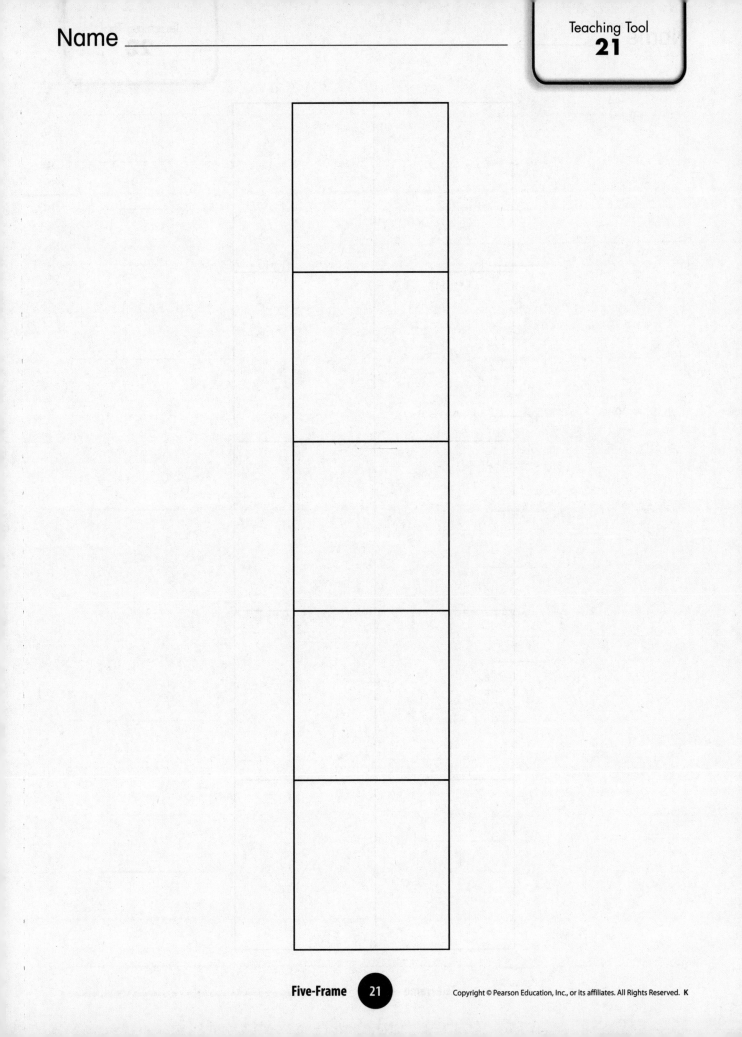

Name _____

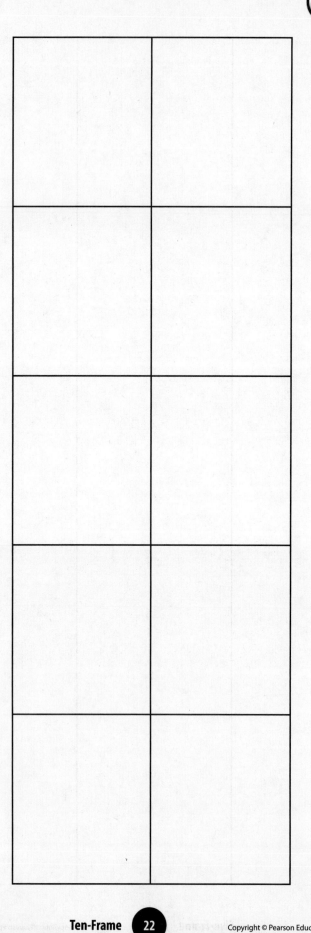

Ten-Frame **22**

Name _____

Double Ten-Frame **23**

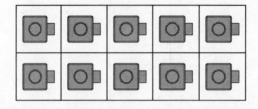

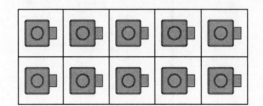

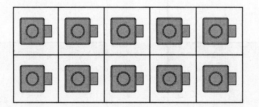

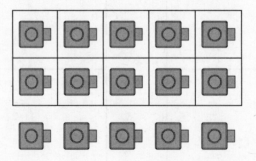

Name _____

Part-Part Mat 26

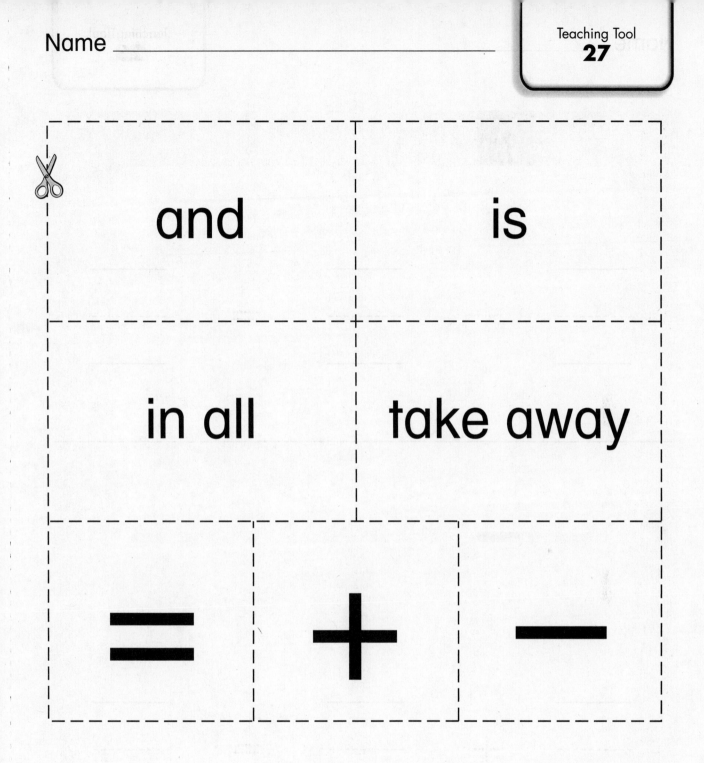

and

is

in all

take away

＝

＋

−

_____   .....   _____   :::::::   _____

- - - - - - -   - - - - - -   - - - - - -

_____   _____   _____

_____

_____   .....   _____   :::::::   _____

- - - - - - -   - - - - - -   - - - - - -

_____   _____   _____

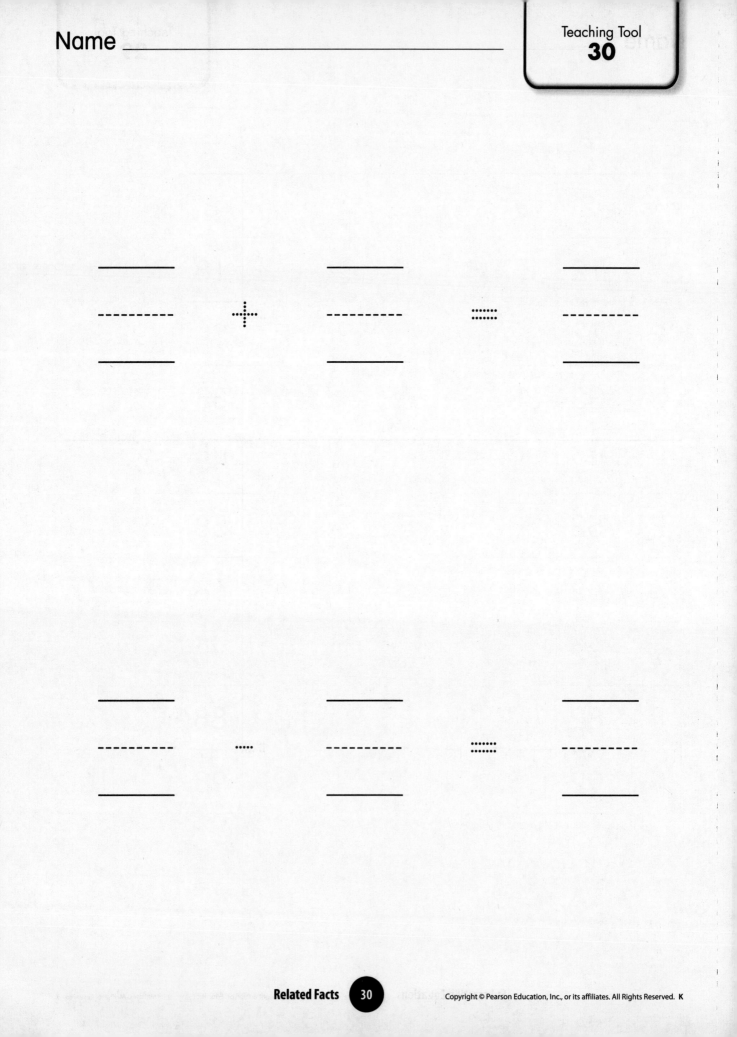

1	2	3	4	5	6	7	8	9	10
11	12	13	14	15	16	17	18	19	20
21	22	23	24	25	26	27	28	29	30
31	32	33	34	35	36	37	38	39	40
41	42	43	44	45	46	47	48	49	50
51	52	53	54	55	56	57	58	59	60
61	62	63	64	65	66	67	68	69	70
71	72	73	74	75	76	77	78	79	80
81	82	83	84	85	86	87	88	89	90
91	92	93	94	95	96	97	98	99	100

Name _____

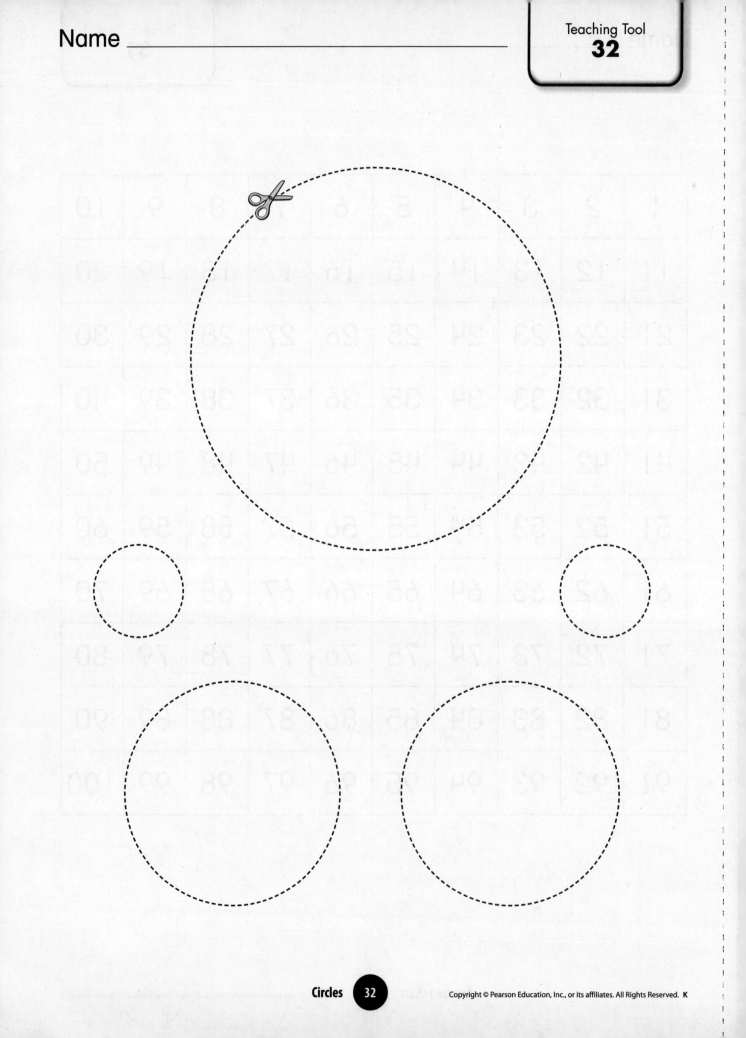

Name _____

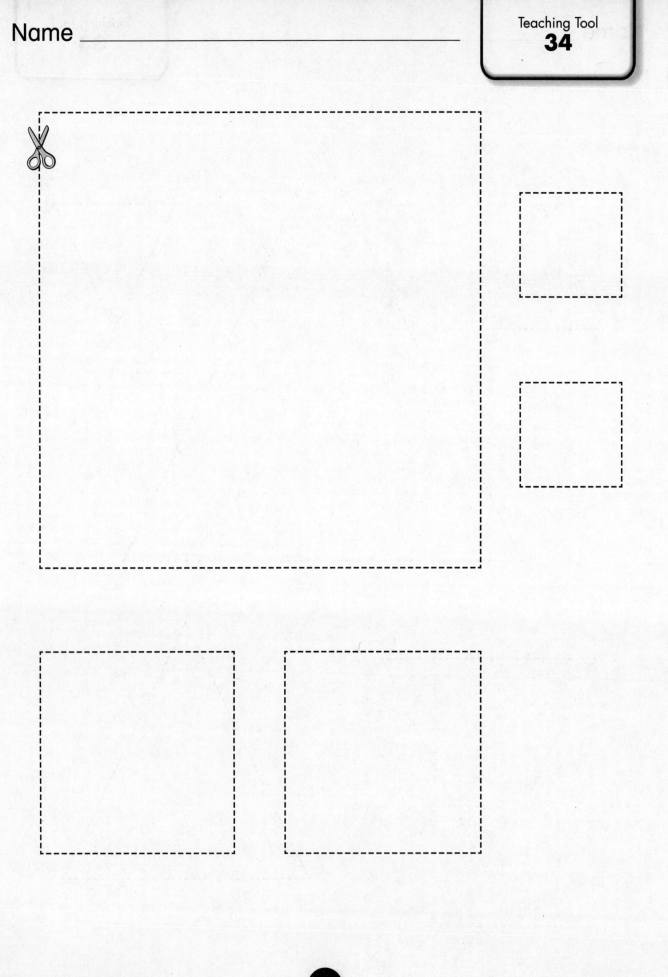

Name _____

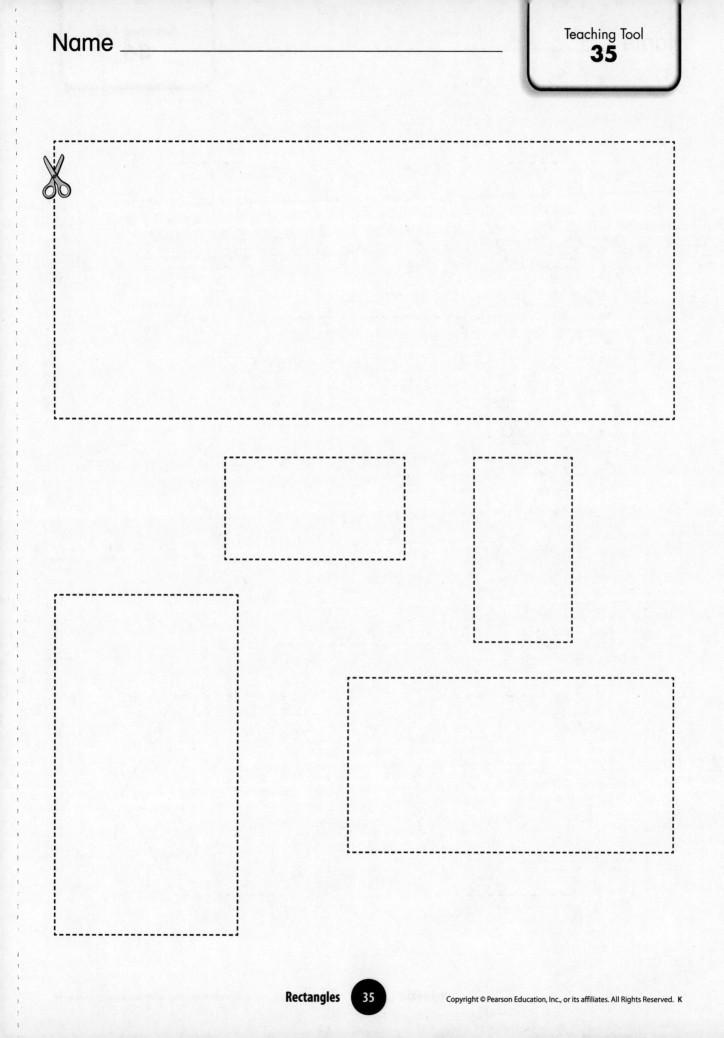

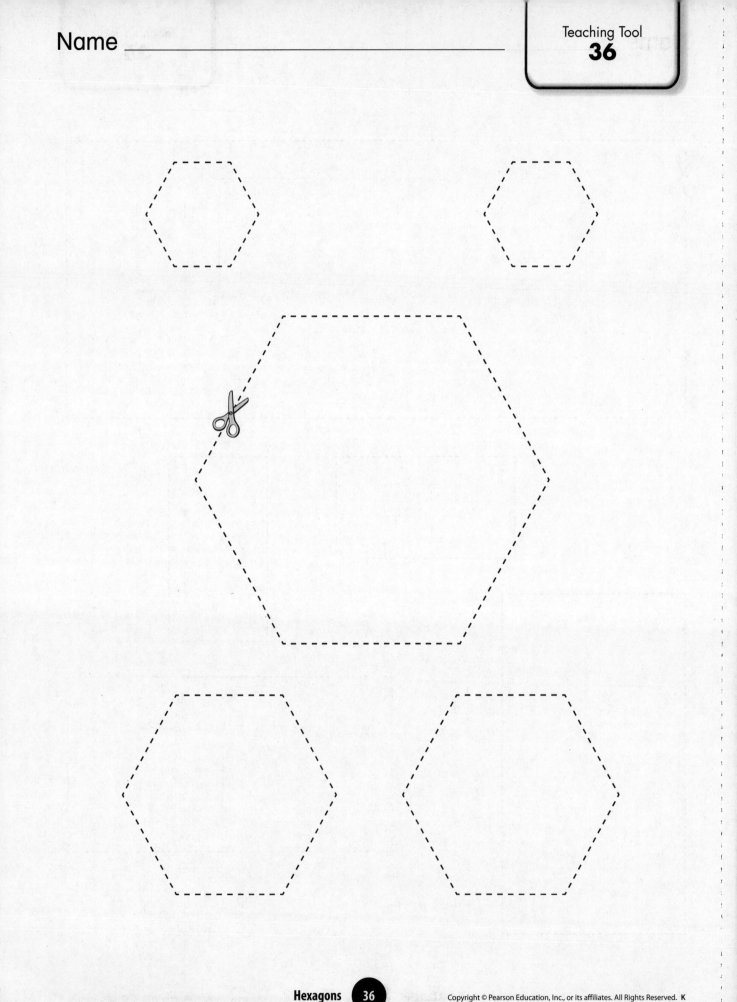

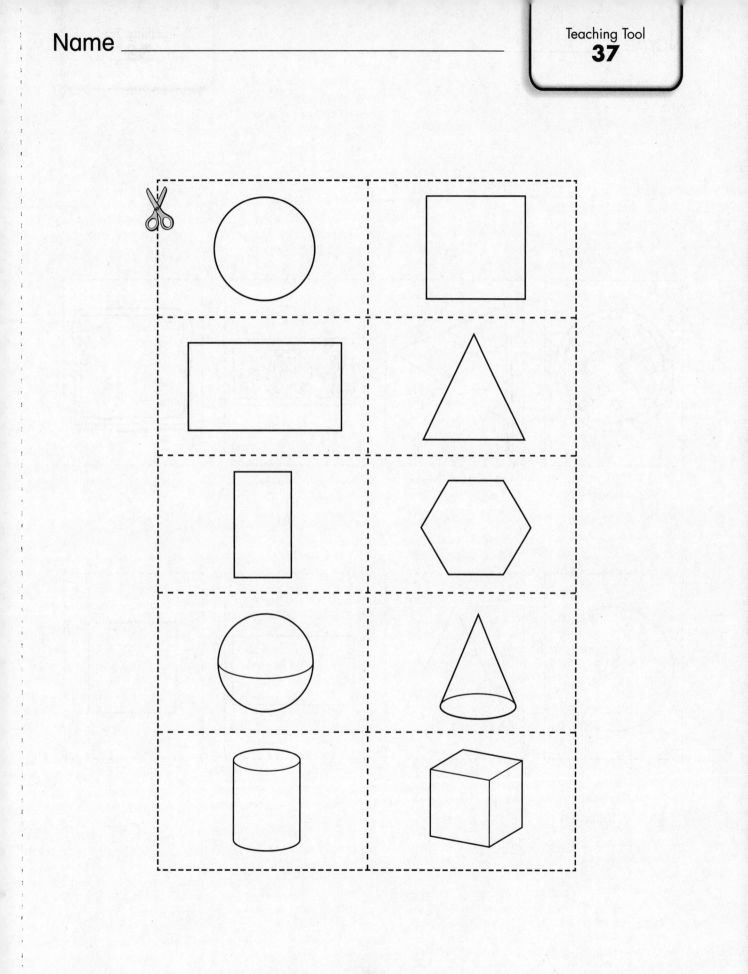

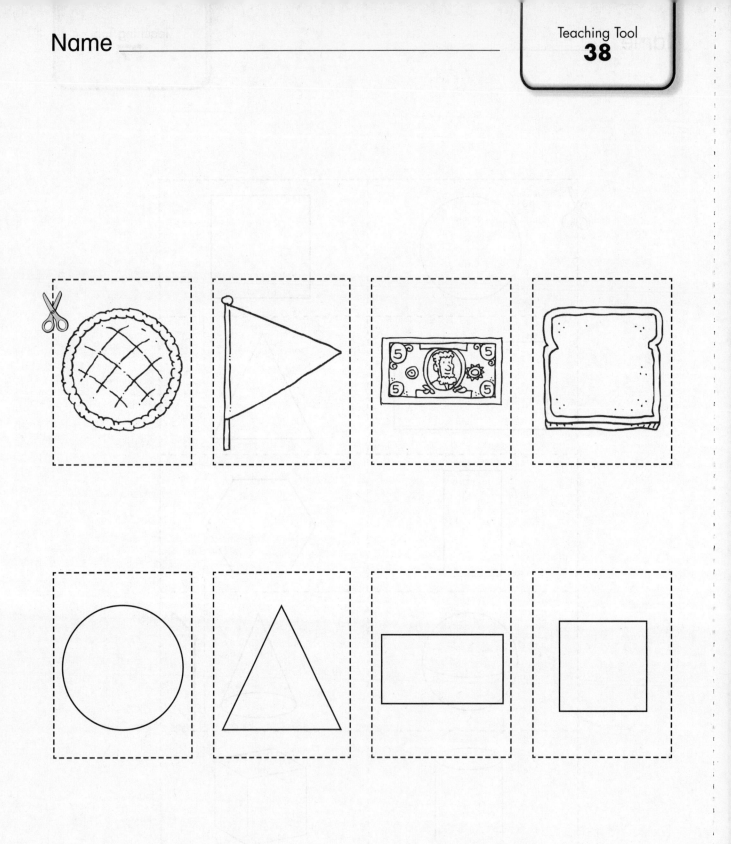

Name _____

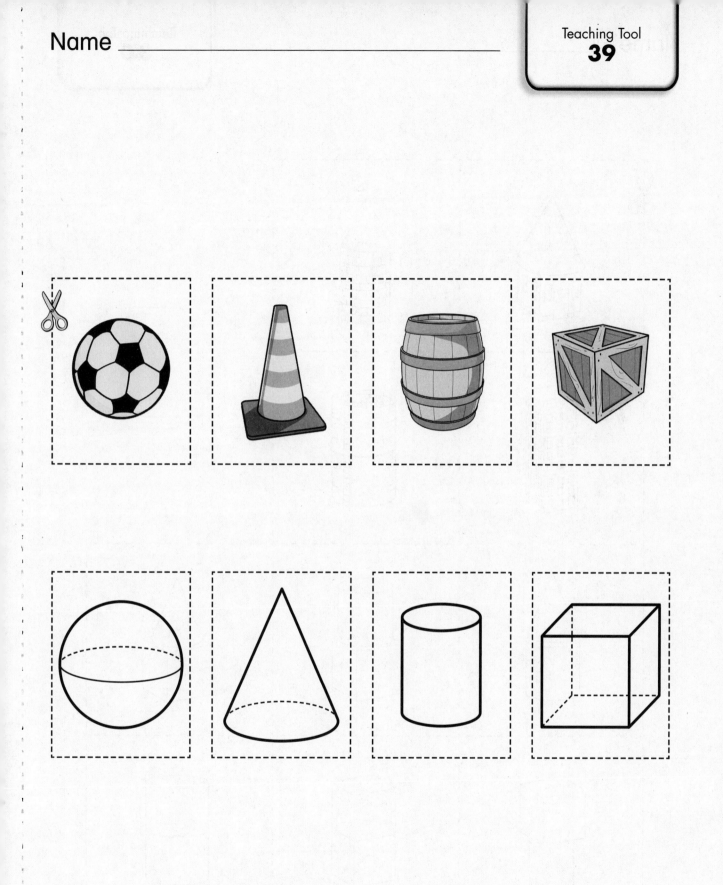

Name _____

Building with Solid Figures 40

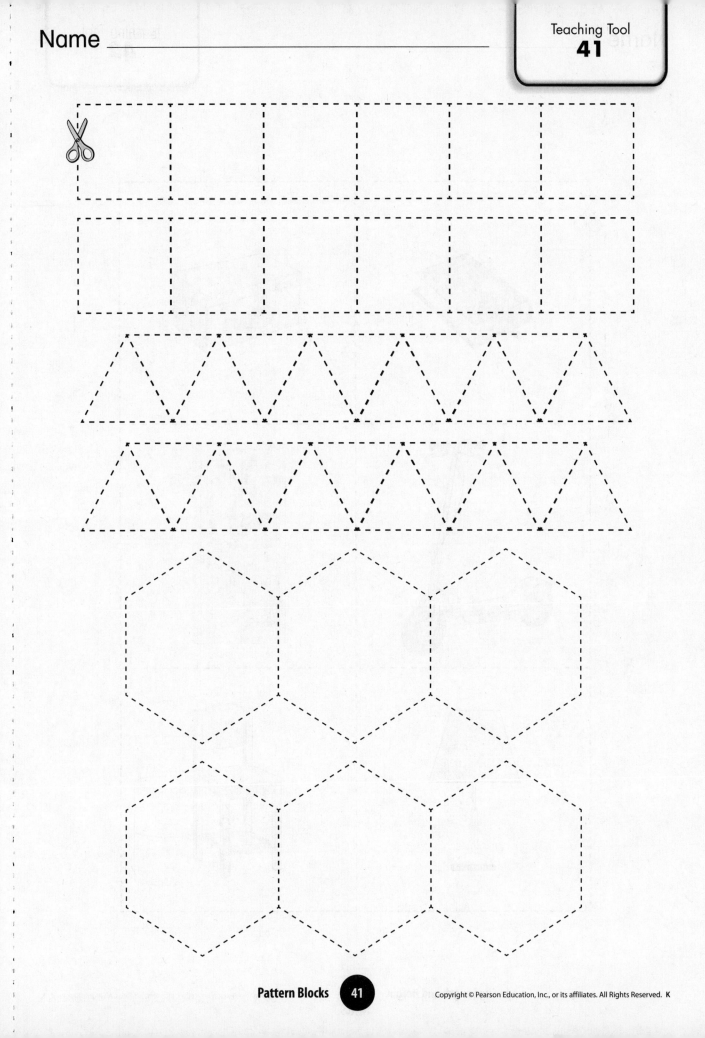

Name ______________________________

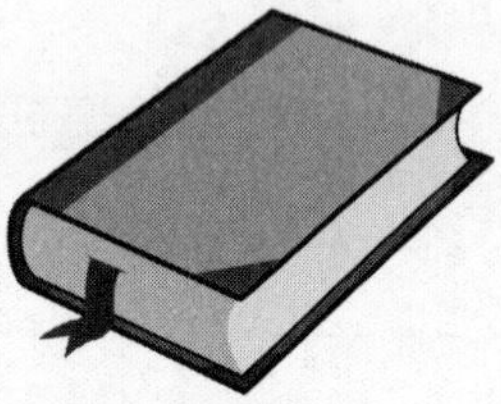

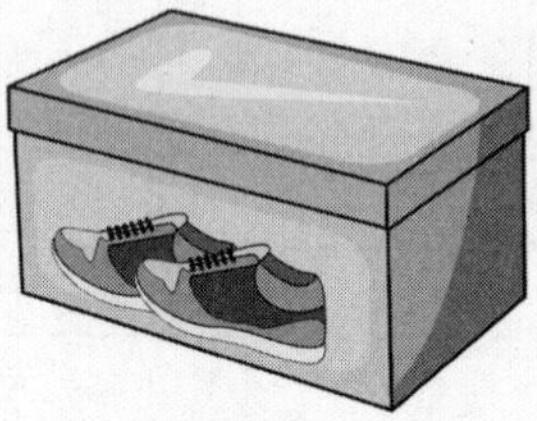

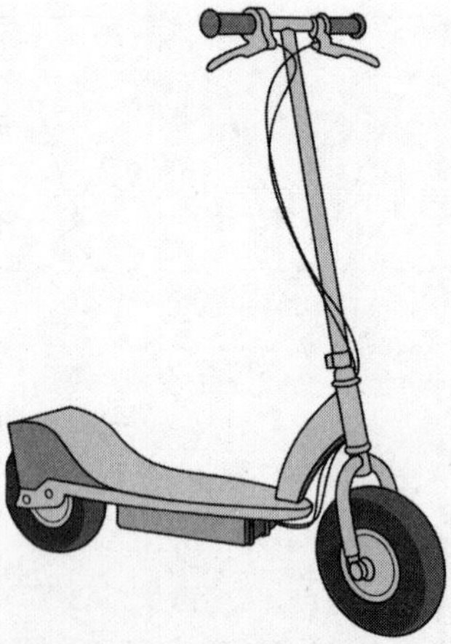

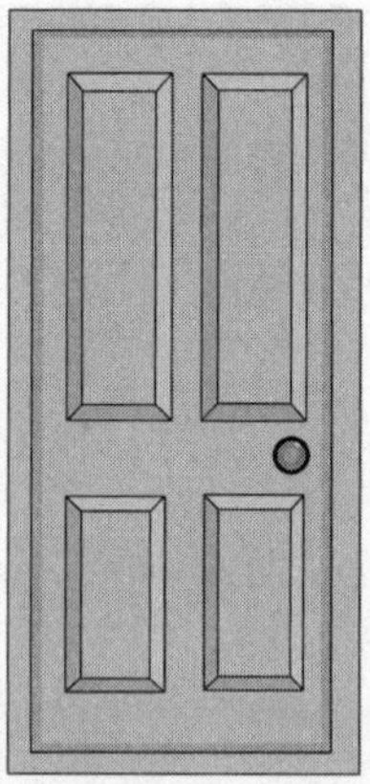

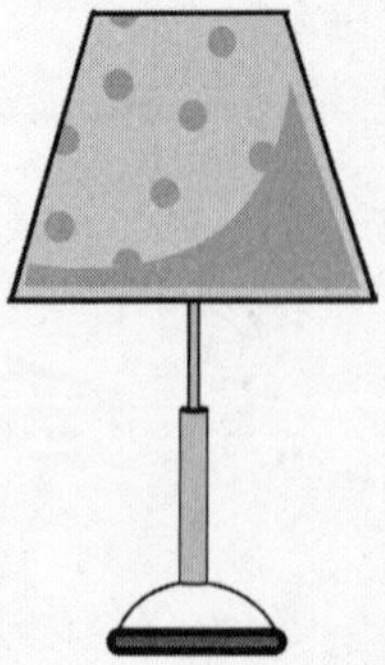

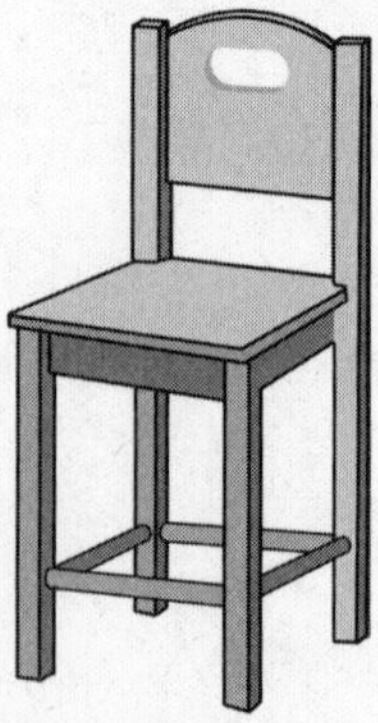

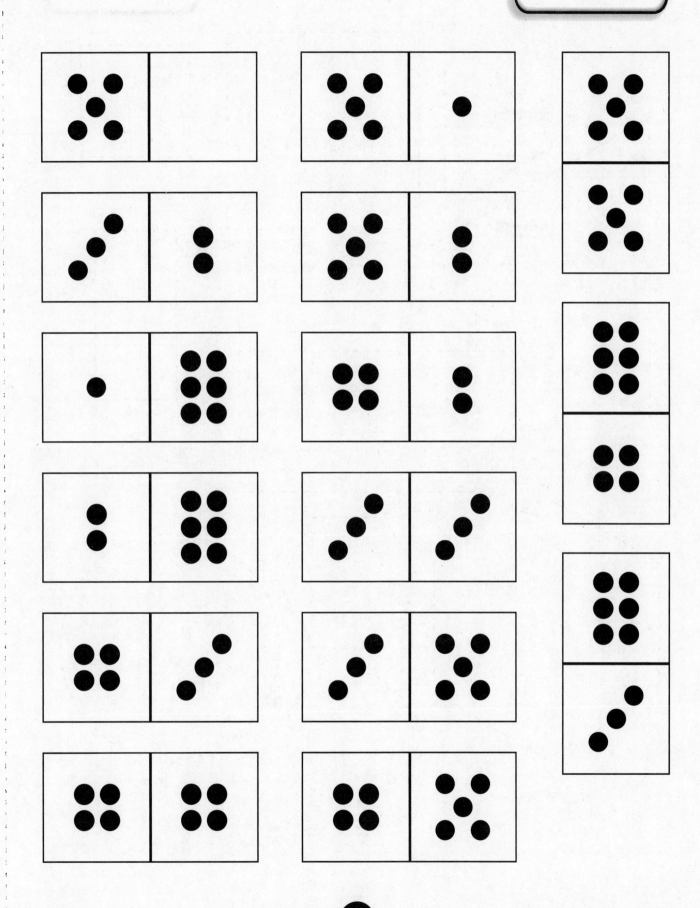

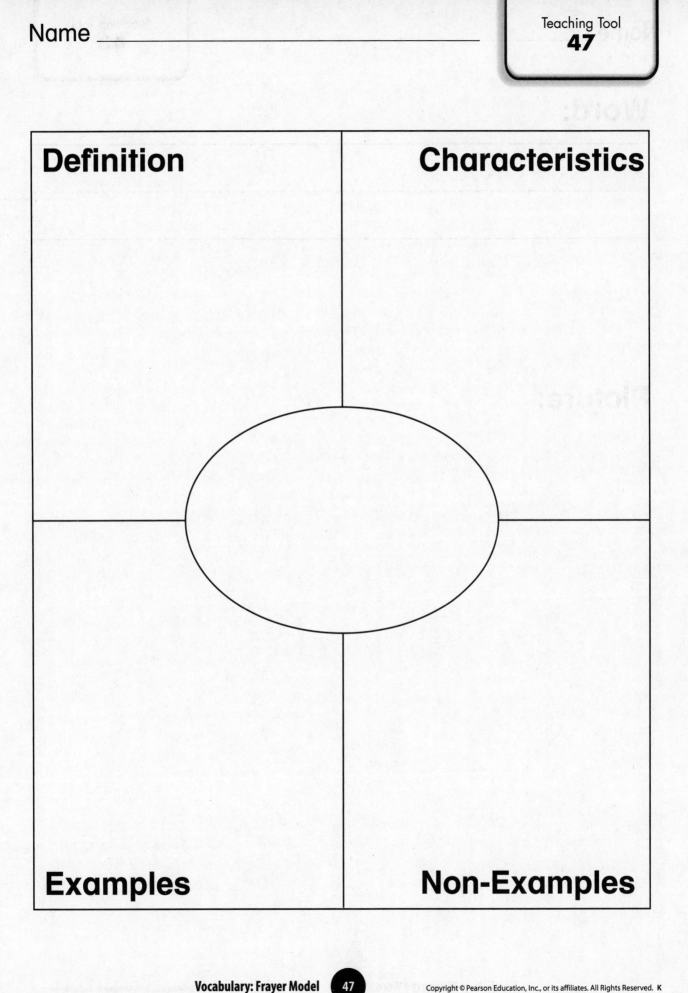

Definition

Characteristics

Examples

Non-Examples

Name _____

Word:

_____

- -

_____

Picture:

New Word	What It Means

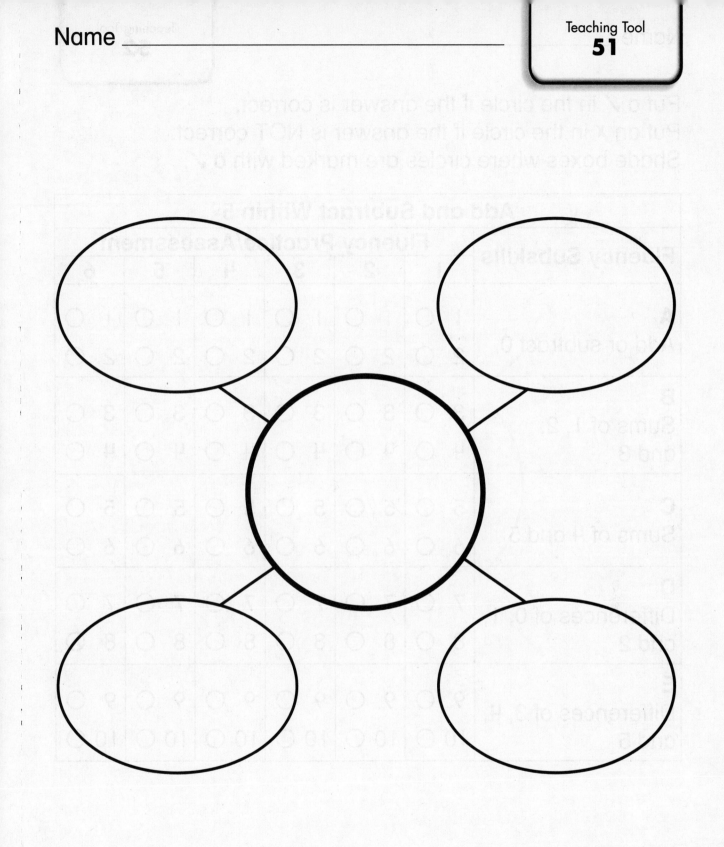

Name _____

Put a ✓ in the circle if the answer is correct.
Put an ✗ in the circle if the answer is NOT correct.
Shade boxes where circles are marked with a ✓.

Add and Subtract Within 5						
Fluency Subskills	**Fluency Practice/Assessment**					
	1	2	3	4	5	6
A Add or subtract 0.	1 ○ 2 ○	1 ○ 2 ○	1 ○ 2 ○	1 ○ 2 ○	1 ○ 2 ○	1 ○ 2 ○
B Sums of 1, 2, and 3	3 ○ 4 ○	3 ○ 4 ○	3 ○ 4 ○	3 ○ 4 ○	3 ○ 4 ○	3 ○ 4 ○
C Sums of 4 and 5	5 ○ 6 ○	5 ○ 6 ○	5 ○ 6 ○	5 ○ 6 ○	5 ○ 6 ○	5 ○ 6 ○
D Differences of 0, 1, and 2	7 ○ 8 ○	7 ○ 8 ○	7 ○ 8 ○	7 ○ 8 ○	7 ○ 8 ○	7 ○ 8 ○
E Differences of 3, 4, and 5	9 ○ 10 ○	9 ○ 10 ○	9 ○ 10 ○	9 ○ 10 ○	9 ○ 10 ○	9 ○ 10 ○

Name _____

+	0	1	2	3	4	5
0	0	1	2	3	4	5
1	1	2	3	4	5	
2	2	3	4	5		
3	3	4	5			
4	4	5				
5	5					

Addition Table 53

Name _____

Self-Assessment Tool

I am on the road to understanding...

Mark an X on the road to show where you are.

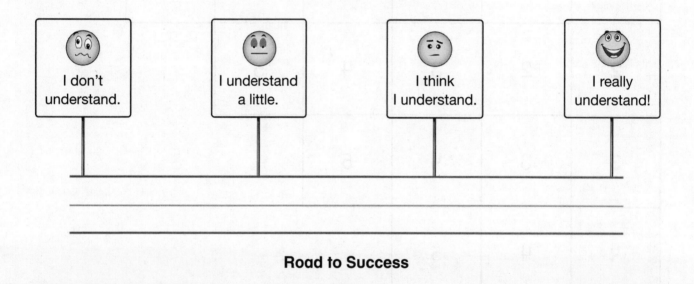

I don't understand.

I understand a little.

I think I understand.

I really understand!

Road to Success

Explain the choice you made above.

To the teacher: Read the directions to the students. Let students respond orally, as needed.